Cambridge Elements

Elements in Women in Music
edited by
Rhiannon Mathias
Bangor University

BANDLEADER MRS MARY HAMER AND HER BOYS

Popular Music and Dance Cultures in Interwar Liverpool

Laura Hamer
The Open University

Michael Brocken
Independent Scholar

CAMBRIDGE UNIVERSITY PRESS

Shaftesbury Road, Cambridge CB2 8EA, United Kingdom

One Liberty Plaza, 20th Floor, New York, NY 10006, USA

477 Williamstown Road, Port Melbourne, VIC 3207, Australia

314–321, 3rd Floor, Plot 3, Splendor Forum, Jasola District Centre, New Delhi – 110025, India

103 Penang Road, #05–06/07, Visioncrest Commercial, Singapore 238467

Cambridge University Press is part of Cambridge University Press & Assessment, a department of the University of Cambridge.

We share the University's mission to contribute to society through the pursuit of education, learning and research at the highest international levels of excellence.

www.cambridge.org
Information on this title: www.cambridge.org/9781009486941

DOI: 10.1017/9781009388832

© Laura Hamer and Michael Brocken 2025

This publication is in copyright. Subject to statutory exception and to the provisions of relevant collective licensing agreements, no reproduction of any part may take place without the written permission of Cambridge University Press & Assessment.

When citing this work, please include a reference to the DOI 10.1017/9781009388832

First published 2025

A catalogue record for this publication is available from the British Library

ISBN 978-1-009-48694-1 Hardback
ISBN 978-1-009-38885-6 Paperback
ISSN 2633-6871 (online)
ISSN 2633-6863 (print)

Cambridge University Press & Assessment has no responsibility for the persistence or accuracy of URLs for external or third-party internet websites referred to in this publication and does not guarantee that any content on such websites is, or will remain accurate or appropriate.

For EU product safety concerns, contact us at Calle de José Abascal, 56, 1°, 28003 Madrid, Spain, or email eugpsr@cambridge.org

Bandleader Mrs Mary Hamer and Her Boys

Popular Music and Dance Cultures in Interwar Liverpool

Elements in Women in Music

DOI: 10.1017/9781009388832
First published online: March 2025

Laura Hamer
The Open University

Michael Brocken
Independent Scholar

Author for correspondence: Laura Hamer, laura.hamer@open.ac.uk

Abstract: The city of Liverpool is renowned for its popular music, although the formidable hagiography which has developed around the Beatles tends to dominate historical considerations to the virtual exclusion of the many other varied genres which have flourished in the city before, during, and after them. Within Liverpool's popular-music past is a partially hidden history of women's musical leadership. This Element concerns the Grafton Rooms' bandleader, dancer, and pianist Mary Hamer (1904–1992). Hamer led the otherwise all-male dance band at the Grafton for two decades, providing dancers with first-class dance music. The Element considers Hamer within the rapidly evolving dance music culture of interwar Liverpool, and discusses the different genres and sub-genres of popular music and dance presented at the Grafton and the role(s) of women in popular music and as bandleaders. This is contextualised within the contemporary social anxieties of popular dance cultures, sexuality, faith, class, and race.

Keywords: Mary Hamer, Women bandleaders, Interwar Liverpool, British dance music, The Grafton Rooms

© Laura Hamer and Michael Brocken 2025

ISBNs: 9781009486941 (HB), 9781009388856 (PB), 9781009388832 (OC)
ISSNs: 2633-6871 (online), 2633-6863 (print)

Contents

1 Introduction: Uncovering a Hidden Popular Music History of Liverpool   1

2 British Dance Music Culture and Interwar Social Anxieties   9

3 Dancers, Musicians, and Managers: Creating Mr Malcolm Munro, Marie Daly, and Wilf Hamer   20

4 Move to the Grafton Rooms: Old Tyme Nights and the Built Environment   37

5 Taking over the Band: Mrs Wilf Hamer and Her Boys, Strategies of Female Dance Band Leadership   51

6 Conclusion: Gender, Genre, and Looking beyond the Beatles   65

Bibliography   67

1 Introduction: Uncovering a Hidden Popular Music History of Liverpool

An enthusiastic critic writing in *Tune Times* in October 1934 proclaimed that:

> One of Liverpool's leading ballrooms [the Grafton Rooms] is spotlighting Wilf Hamer and his Band for the winter season. Will [sic] obliged me with a workout of the band's pet numbers, and gave the impression of strong ensemble specialisation [...] well up to the London standard [...] The management is a model of efficiency, and I have no doubt that this is due to no other than Mr. Malcolm Munro, who looks genial, sounds genial, and has a genuine and genial regard for the band.[1]

This review highlights the high regard in which Wilf Hamer and his band, Malcolm Munro, and the Grafton Rooms were held in the 1930s. Unmentioned in this particular extract, but equally well thought of, was Mary Hamer (born Daly also known as Marie, 1904–1992), professional exhibition ballroom dancer, pianist, and danceband leader. They have all become part of a hidden history of Liverpool's popular music past. The reasons for this are complex, yet pressing amongst them is the fact that few popular music historians take little more than a passing interest in any of the diverse forms of popular music that flourished in Liverpool before the Beatles, especially when they involved women as active, rather than passive, participants.[2]

This Element seeks to redress this by focussing upon the rich dance music culture which flourished at the Grafton Rooms – one of Liverpool's most salubrious and well-known venues for ballroom dancing – from the 1920s until the mid-1950s, and of the vital part played by Mary Hamer. Alongside Malcolm Munro (1887–1971), the manager of the Grafton Rooms, Wilf Hamer (1907–1936), the leader of the Grafton Rooms' house band from 1928 until his death in 1936, Mary Hamer was also a key figure within our narrative. Mary Hamer was professionally active under her own name, Mary Daly (sometimes given professionally as Marie), until the death of her first husband in 1936. Following this, she was known as Mrs Mary Hamer. Here, she is referred to as Mary Hamer in Sections 1, 2, 5, and 6, and as Mary Daly in Sections 3 and 4.

---

[1] Anonymous, 'Liverpool', *Tune Times* (October 1934), 66.
[2] For an important study of other popular music cultures in Liverpool, see Michael Brocken, *Other Voices: Hidden Histories of Liverpool's Popular Music Scenes, 1930s–1970s* (Farnham: Ashgate, 2010). For two other major studies of popular music in Liverpool beyond the Beatles – although they do not directly touch on dance music culture or any popular music prior to the Second World War – see Sara Cohen, *Decline, Renewal and the City in Popular Music Culture: Beyond the Beatles* (Farnham: Ashgate, 2007) and Marion Leonard and Robert Strachan, *The Beat Goes On: Liverpool, Popular Music and the Changing City* (Liverpool: Liverpool University Press, 2010).

The Varying Contexts of This Research Project

The research upon which this Element is based has occupied us, albeit intermittently, for several years. We first began work upon it in 2015, when we were both working in the Music Department of Liverpool Hope University. We were initially inspired by a telephone call from Mrs Audrey McKinnell, who was looking for a new home for the extensive record collection of her late husband, Frank.[3] Both Audrey, who was crazy about ballroom dancing during her youth in the late 1930s and 1940s, and Frank had been regulars at the Grafton Rooms, West Derby Road, Liverpool, and Audrey remembered Mary Hamer very well both as an extremely accomplished ballroom dancer and as the leader of the renowned Grafton dance band. Audrey, therefore, became the first person who we interviewed concerning Mary Hamer, the dancing, and the music at the Grafton Rooms.[4]

The research process accelerated somewhat in August 2016 when we were contacted by Mary Hamer's youngest son – George Hamer – who got in touch after he realised that we were conducting research on his mother. Contact with George quickly led to our meeting a few of Mary Hamer's other surviving relatives, including her grandson Henry (who at that time worked as Community Engagement Officer for Everton Football Club) and her niece Margaret (who grew up with her great uncle John, better known under the professional name of 'Malcolm Munro': the Grafton Room's talented venue manager). This contact with the family led to a great deal of helpful information, much of which archival research alone had not previously revealed, and to an extremely important discovery. As it turned out, in Margaret's house in Southport reposed a suitcase full of primary sources from the Grafton Rooms, all long cherished by the family. The suitcase also included a source which, for more than twenty years previously, Mike had been searching: Malcolm Munro's unpublished autobiography, entitled *Dancing Mad: An Autographical Dancing Diary*.[5] The manuscript had barely reached an edit state, having been typed by the author and sent to a reader/copy editor, a Mr Richard Whittington Egan, for a report on its viability as a published text. Whittington Egan considered the work 'first-rate' but then went on to discuss revisions of the text before an approach to a publisher was made: 'Spelling, sequence, punctuation and

---

[3] The Frank McKinnell Collection subsequently became the bedrock of what was then the Popular Music Resources Centre at Liverpool Hope University.

[4] The early stages of our research were also developed through the opportunity to present conference papers on Mary Hamer and the Grafton Rooms in Liverpool, Birmingham, Bangor, Dublin, Tromsø, and London. We are grateful to everyone who offered generous feedback and suggestions.

[5] In writing a dance autobiography it is likely that Munro was inspired by similar well-known dancer colleagues of his era. Well-known examples include Josephine Baker's *Dancing through Life* (London: Hollis & Carter, 1947) and Victor Silvester's *Dancing Is My Life: The Autobiography of Victor Silvester* (London: Heinemann, 1958).

paragraphing must also be completely revised and I would further suggest the division of the material into chapters. I have partially corrected the first few pages, but I have been severely hampered in this because of the fact that the typescript is not adequately spaced for purposes of correction.'[6] From our study of the manuscript, we believe that Munro worked upon it during the later 1950s and into the 1960s, completing it around 1968. This Element draws directly upon the unpublished manuscript of *Dancing Mad*, and upon the hitherto unstudied family archive materials.

Towards an Interdisciplinary Study of Music and Dance

The early twentieth century represents one of the most innovative and diverse periods in the history of Western dance genres, both performative and social. From the perspective of performative dance, ballet – through the innovations of such visionary dance companies as the *Ballets russes* and the *Ballets suédois* – developed from the conservative art form it had fossilised into by the later nineteenth century and blossomed into an experimental one; whilst pioneering solo female dancers, such as Isadora Duncan, Loïe Fuller, and Josephine Baker became icons of the age. Social dance also developed rapidly during the earlier twentieth century, with regular ballroom imports to Europe from America, including such new dances as the Grizzly Bear, Turkey Trot, One-Step, Fox Trot, Charleston, Slow Waltz, and Lindy Hop (later known as the Jitterbug). In Britain, folk dance also enjoyed a considerable revival. Dance scholarship of the period, however, has tended to privilege theatrical dance genres, and earlier twentieth-century social dance – especially ballroom – has attracted significantly less attention.[7] Academic studies of dance music culture in interwar Britain, meanwhile, tend to consider *either* the music *or* the dance in isolation. This Element seeks to move away from considering the 'dance' and the 'music' components of dance music separately, by striving for an interdisciplinary approach, reflective of Mary Hamer's dual professional identity as *both* dancer *and* musician, and the obvious ways in which she allowed her embodied experiences as a ballroom dancer to influence her approach as a danceband leader.

---

[6] Richard Whittington Egan, 'Report on MSS. Submitted by Mr Malcolm Munro' (c.late 1960s); Hamer-Munro family archives.

[7] An important exception is Rishona Zimring's *Social Dance and the Modernist Imagination in Interwar Britain* (Farnham: Ashgate, 2013). Zimring's study, however, specifically focuses upon the relationship between social dance (embracing both ballroom and the contemporary folk-dance revival) and literary modernism during the period. Theresa Buckland's *Society Dancing: Fashionable Bodies in England, 1870–1920* (Basingstoke: Palgrave Macmillan, 2011), meanwhile, is an important study of the development of ballroom genres in the years immediately preceding the interwar period.

Centring Liverpool

Previous accounts of the development of dance band music in the UK have tended to focus upon London.[8] Although London's status as capital city and role in setting trends that were widely copied elsewhere – in addition to its well-established dance culture and theatres (which often imported American shows) – does provide some justification for the logic of this, it also creates London-centric historical narratives which tend to ignore the importance of what was happening elsewhere. Through concentrating upon Liverpool – a transient port city with well-established and diverse venues for popular entertainment that had grown up to cater for the city's very different demographics (which included a range of ethnicities), and strong links with the United States – this study offers a revisionist investigation into the development of popular music and dance in the UK, which highlights the importance of Liverpool.

Considerations of Liverpool's popular music histories, of course, face their own substantial challenge in the shape of the Beatles. In the histories of twentieth-century popular music, Liverpool has been rewritten, re-invented, and re-historicised as a city utterly dominated by male-oriented binary and at times racialised narratives concerning not only the Beatles and Merseybeat, but also those of us who were influenced by the same. So much does this perspective pervade our popular music histories (or should that be mythologies?) that the genres, venues, music businesses, and experiences that existed prior to and post the emergence of rock 'n' roll in the city have been largely ignored by historians of popular music who take an interest in the city of Liverpool. For example, the case of Liverpool-born jazz pioneer Gordon Stretton (1887–1983) is most illustrative in respect of the gross lack of attention afforded to those successful artists who precede the Beatles by some decades. Brocken and Daniels propose that:

---

[8] Catherine Tackley's seminal study of the development of British jazz, Catherine Parsonage, *The Evolution of Jazz in Britain, 1880–1935* (Aldershot: Ashgate, 2005), for instance, focuses upon London. Tackley is currently working on a project entitled 'The British Dance Band: Music and Musicians in the Mainstream' funded by a Leverhulme Major Research Fellowship which broadens the British dance band remit to include other important towns and cities throughout the UK. Jim Godbolt's *A History of Jazz in Britain, 1919–1950*, Revised Edition (London: Northway Books, 2005) also pays little attention to Liverpool (and none at all to the Grafton Rooms). James J. Nott's *Music for the People: Popular Music and Dance in Interwar Britain* (Oxford: Oxford University Press, 2002) provides an important overview of dance music culture, and he does refer to dance halls in Liverpool, the Grafton Rooms, and Malcolm Munro, as does his important focused study on the palais de danse during the interwar period: James J. Nott, *Going to the Palais: A Social and Cultural Study of Dancing and Dance Halls in Britain, 1918–1960* (Oxford: Oxford University Press, 2015). Unlike our study, however, which focuses upon one specific case study, Nott's books draw upon diverse examples from throughout the UK. Tricia Jenkins' short book, *'Let's Go Dancing': Dance Band Memories of 1930s Liverpool*, Liverpool Sound Series (Liverpool: University of Liverpool Press/Institute of Popular Music, 1994), currently offers the only detailed study of dance music culture in 1930's Liverpool. This is an extremely slim volume, however, and in no ways offers an in-depth study.

[aside from the fact that he was Black] Gordon Stretton is also hidden from historical view in Liverpool by the advent of rock 'n' roll, Merseybeat, and, more specifically, the Beatles. He preceded the development of these later Liverpool popular music events by several decades, therefore is largely discounted, locally. Few local or national popular music historians have taken more than a passing interest in any forms of popular music emanating from Liverpudlians prior to the Beatles – whether that be the Black Gordon Stretton or (say) the white female dance band leader at the Grafton Rooms in the city, Mary Hamer.[9]

As with Gordon Stretton, only snippets of information exist concerning Mary Hamer's historical contributions to popular music history. Despite her great popularity (not only in Liverpool), her awareness of popular tastes in dance music, her frequent radio broadcasts for the BBC, and her successes as a dancer, musician, and bandleader, Mary Hamer is most certainly a partially hidden historical figure.

Mary Hamer's musical career actually overlapped early Merseybeat trajectories; furthermore, the venue with which she has become most associated, the Grafton Rooms, also played host to several important Merseybeat and rock 'n' roll shows during the rise of this popular music scene. However, it is probably correct to state that owing to Liverpool's own place-based narrative concerning popular music, Mary Hamer's successes will (knowingly or otherwise) always be measured oddly *in contradistinction* with those of the Beatles and their fellow Merseybeat-based artistes. The fact also remains that Beatles histories vis-à-vis Liverpool can still be grossly inaccurate and in many cases – especially since the rise of Beatles tourism in the city – myth has taken over from well-researched history. So much so in fact, that one can now historicise the creation and development processes of those very myths, in relation to the Beatles tourism industry.[10] Further, Beatles writers tend to codify the group's emergence as a kind of 'year zero' historical event (as John Lennon is frequently [mis]quoted regarding the statement 'before Elvis there was nothing') – but this simply cannot be so.

The histories of Liverpool also inform us that, as a global imperialist centre, the city has a corporate hubris surrounding its apparent cosmopolitanism. However, this civic hubris-cum-myth has permeated the city to such an extent that a wide variety of different and perhaps more complex artistic traits have been largely ignored – particularly in relation to popular tastes that do not quite 'fit' either Liverpool's view of itself or the popular music narratives that concentrate almost exclusively on beat groups. As Brocken states in his

---

[9] Michael Brocken and Jeff Daniels, *Gordon Stretton, Black British Transoceanic Jazz Pioneer – A New Jazz Chronicle* (London: Lexington, 2018), 255.

[10] For example, see Michael Brocken, *The 21st Century Legacy of the Beatles: Liverpool and Popular Music Heritage Tourism* (Farnham: Ashgate, 2015).

previous study of the other forms of popular music which have flourished within Liverpool, *Other Voices*:

> The varying and variable popular music scenes that existed in twentieth century Liverpool (of interest to all popular music historians quite simply because they were important to those involved) reveal a great deal. They were among the most important symbols of change and statis in the shifting cultural temperatures of mid-twentieth century Liverpool, being representations of race, class, gender, sexuality, economics, authenticity, and affect. It is usually acknowledged that this was indeed the case for rock 'n' roll, but it is seldom revealed that, for example, country music, the cabaret or folk 'scenes' performed similar duties – so why not? [...] The very complexity of such diachronic and synchronic behaviours and meanings should not be ignored [i.e., for the sake of the Beatles].[11]

Each generation quite naturally feels that *their* experiences were unique and for those involved they most certainly were. However, our roles as historians should always include attempts to capture feelings as openly as we can – we should not be predisposed to define reception and states of mind by commerce, gender or contemporary political binarisms. This is where redaction criticism can be very useful to the popular music historian, for the researcher can see how the ongoing writing of Liverpool histories are in fact rather like movements of strata through time, in which the historical writing reflects the period of time in which the writing takes place, rather than the subject matter under investigation.

So, there will always be grounds for questioning whether certain popular music activities (whatever they happen to be) were in fact truly characteristic of any so-called 'era'. In terms of Mary Hamer and the Grafton Rooms we might remind ourselves that popular music eras always coalesce and overlap – they are never discrete. For example, at different times in the post–Second World War 'era' the Grafton Rooms accommodated both Mary Hamer and Her Boys *and* Merseybeat. It is also perhaps worth proposing that many popular music eras and genres tend to pass by just as many people as they apparently embrace and they cannot be discussed as being in any way 'globally' definitive (as is often suggested in relation to 'jazz'). We are now able to provide 'archive-as-critique', bibliographies, oral histories, interview transcriptions, and so on, all of which allow us to [re]consider previous popular music texts in a relatively hermeneutic way. All such 'voices' are grounded in subject-based historical 'realities' and cannot be lumped together via pen-based subjectivities, especially those determined by historical writings previously deemed to be 'the last word'.

---

[11] Brocken, *Other Voices*, 6–7.

The recording of micro-contexts openly challenges texts that have previously glossed over reception strategies in micro-circumstances. As Lawrence Grossberg has stated: 'The fan can only be understood historically, as located in a set of different possible relations to culture. In fact, everyone is constantly a fan of various sorts of things, for one cannot exist in a world where nothing matters (including the fact that nothing matters).'[12] Therefore the continual reinvention of popular music studies via our concentration upon micro-topics, individual interpretive strategies and previously marginalised histories will inevitably challenge preceding canonic narratives and reinvent the ways in which we conduct our research. As a discipline, popular music studies should continue to be *directly* associated with issues relating to an ongoing discourse of reassessment and modification. Such a position reflects an organic, ongoing unity of resistance to the closing down of debate and presents alternative readings that question the validity of residual histories within a canon of limited and binary discourses.

Returning to Mary Hamer and the Grafton

Studies of popular music media fandom have been extremely productive areas of research that have assisted in bringing partially hidden voices into historical relief perhaps for the first time. They have created awareness of distinctive worlds 'founded less upon the consumption of pre-existing texts [and more upon] the production of fan texts which draw raw materials from the media as a basis for new forms of cultural creation'.[13] Such proactive audience creativities have more recently been characterised as the product of intelligent, cognitive receivers, rather than the outpourings of exploited worshipful fans. It should be clear to all researchers of popular music that fans are always proactive, discriminatory, and decisive. For instance, Audrey McKinnell informed us that:

> Mary [Hamer] was able to create an entire world for me, but funnily enough it was never quite the same elsewhere: so, the Grafton must also have contributed to that feeling I got of being in another world but also secure. I remember Frank [Audrey's husband] and I being on holiday in North Wales one summer and Mary and her Boys were resident at one of the Welsh ballrooms[14] – can't remember which one now but it was a stunning place and I know it's long

---

[12] Lawrence Grossberg, 'Is There a Fan in the House? The Affective Sensibility of Fandom', in Lisa A. Lewis (ed.), *The Adoring Audience: Fan Culture and Popular Media* (London: Routledge, 1992), 63.

[13] Henry Jenkins, 'Strangers No More We Sing': Filking and the Social Construction of the Science Fiction Fan Community', in Lisa A. Lewis (ed.), *The Adoring Audience: Fan Culture and Popular Media* (London: Routledge, 1992), 82.

[14] This was most likely the Queen's Dance Hall in Rhyl or else Payne's Majestic in Llandudno.

gone. So, we went along, and it was a really good night! but somehow it just wasn't the same as being at the Grafton. And it's no use you asking me why it wasn't the same because I don't really know why, except that maybe it was because we were in a different place rather than 'our' place. So, for us the magic was to do with the mixture of both the sound and the place – difficult to explain but we were 'Grafton people', I suppose.[15]

Audrey's observations remain extremely significant to the popular music researcher because they were honest, informed in good faith as an attempt to explain her experiences as a dancer and receiver of the music she loved, and difficult for her to communicate in words. Audrey effectively re-writes history by suggesting that, for her, both the places and spaces *really* mattered. So much so, in fact, that her favourite band did not appear to be quite 'the same' performing at a different ballroom in North Wales. Such subjectivities are extremely important to record for they place the reception of music at the forefront while displacing somewhat overly simplistic historicisations: those which endlessly prioritise the artist in the creation of meaning and affect. If we merely countenance artistic endeavour as a historical one-way communication device, we leave out the co-compositional creativity of the listener. We simply cannot pigeonhole people's reception strategies as if they are/were instructed by the artist. Such concrete totalities fail to explain how experiencing sound works on different levels. Sonic discourses are created as much by receivers 'on the hoof', as they are by musicians, and they cannot be repackaged by historians describing receivers as a lumpen mass of (in this case) dancers. In the past some might have informed Audrey that she was effectively 'kidding herself' and that it was all just part of the way in which the 'business' of popular music exploited her. But such significant experiences cannot be explained away by simplistic one-way communication models.

As far as dancing was concerned, Mary Hamer and Her Boys appealed to innumerable important fascinations of both mind and body: close contact dancing at both the Embassy Rooms (where she led the house band in the 1920s, discussed in Section 3) and the Grafton Rooms might be as sexual as it was 'formal'. When Mary Hamer selected her band's repertoire for an evening's entertainment, what took place on the dancefloor was of primary importance to her – perhaps even a key issue in the survival of the band as a live event: What number comes first? when does the tempo drop? were medleys important? If so, when? which songs or tunes ended a set? how might dancers react to a new dance or tune? and so on. Speaking to Clive Garner of BBC Radio Merseyside in the 1980s she commented about her time at the Embassy Rooms in the early 1920s:

---

[15] Interview with Audrey McKinnell, October 2017.

It was wonderful. Anybody who went to the Embassy Rooms would say so. They would remember the happy days, lovely, they were really nice. I started with the band, but I loved dancing so much that Mr Munro put a piano on the opposite side of the ballroom and I played the piano, and then all the people would come and sit around the piano and ask me to play tunes. It was really lovely.[16]

We will now consider Mary Hamer and her musical environment from this significant dancing-into-bandleading perspective, for we remain convinced that she was one of the most important figures in the history of twentieth-century popular music and dance in the city of Liverpool.

2 British Dance Music Culture and Interwar Social Anxieties

Dancing was the most popular form of entertainment in Britain during the interwar years, rivalled only by the cinema in terms of its wide-spread appeal across all social classes. James J. Nott has coined the useful term 'dance music culture' to describe the dance craze which developed in Britain during this period. As he has commented, '"dance music culture" [...] assumed great importance in the popular culture of the period.'[17] Every major town and city boasted multiple venues for dancing, and Liverpool was no exception. Describing a trip made to the city in the early 1930s, the writer J.B. Priestley waxed lyrical about its nightlife:

> [...] two trams brought me back to the centre of the city, whose essential darkness made a good background for quite a metropolitan display of Neon lighting and flashing signs. Cinemas, theatres (though Liverpool could do with several more), dance-halls, grill-rooms, boxing matches, cocktail bars, all in full glittering swing. The Adelphi Hotel had dressed for the evening, was playing waltzes ...[18]

Priestley's colourful description evokes the richness and the diversity of the popular entertainment available in Liverpool during the interwar period.

As Nott has observed, 'in 1934 Liverpool and Merseyside had "well over" ten public dance halls, a number larger than most, in a city where dancing was one of the most popular pastimes.'[19] He asserts that the most 'important dance halls

---

[16] Mary Hamer to Clive Garner, BBC Radio Merseyside (1980s); cited from Jenkins, *'Let's Go Dancing'*, 40. Clive Garner presented the weekly radio programme *Music and Memories of the 1930s* on BBC Radio Merseyside for more than twenty years. He was a renowned collector/ connoisseur of popular music of the interwar period and held in his collection thousands of recordings and artefacts. Garner got to know Mary Hamer in her old age and spoke with her several times about her career.
[17] Nott, *Music for the People*, 127.
[18] J. B. Priestley, *English Journey* (London: Heinemann, 1934), 249–250.
[19] Nott, *Music for the People*, 158.

in central Liverpool were the Grafton Rooms [...] the Locarno, and the Rialto', and cites Malcolm Munro's estimation (in an interview given to the original Mass Observation Project in 1939) that the weekly attendance at the Grafton Rooms was '4,000 in season compared to 10,000 per week for the Locarno'.[20] Although the Grafton Rooms, the Locarno, the Rialto Ballroom, the Adelphi Hotel, the State Ballroom, and the New Brighton Tower Ballroom (on the Wirral) might have been Liverpool and Merseyside's most up-market dance venues, a whole host of other opportunities for dancing existed. As Tricia Jenkins has commented:

> In the 1930s Liverpool had many dance halls. There were grand places like the Grafton, the Rialto and the State Ballroom but every district had its own small hall used for dances two or three times a week, and every community had its own meeting house or rooms which could be hired for a local hop. Even the Swimming pools, like Garston Baths, could be drained and boarded over for dancing.
>
> Dances were not just held in the evenings. Many people would take an afternoon out to go to a tea dance. There were dinner dances, novelty dances, dancing competitions, dancing schools and cellar parties.[21] There may have been a lot of poverty in Liverpool in the Thirties, but there was also an awful lot of dancing.[22]

This massive vogue for dancing – which was mirrored throughout the UK – did not go unremarked upon in the contemporary press and amongst other social commentators. Despite the huge popularity of both dancing and the popular music which went with it, both provoked considerable social anxieties, much of which focussed upon race, class, and gender. This section considers the contemporary social anxieties associated with interwar dance music culture in order to contextualise the activities, motivations, and receptions of Malcolm Munro, Wilf Hamer, and Mary Hamer.

Dance Music Culture and Interwar Social Anxieties: Race, Class, and Gender

Starting in the 1920s, dance crazes – which had originated in the United States – swept Britain on an almost annual basis. In a society traumatised by war and marked by the abruptly marring simultaneous communal senses of both grief and jubilation, dancing provided an essential escapist function. Thus, dancing became one of the defining pastimes of what has come to be known as the

---

[20] *Ibid.*

[21] The 'cellar parties' to which Jenkins alludes were most associated with Liverpool's Black community.

[22] Jenkins, *'Let's Go Dancing'*, 3.

'roaring twenties'. The African American origins of the new dances, however, prompted considerable anxieties amongst a wide range of contemporary commentators, from writers and journalists to dance teachers. In a society struggling to return to some sense of normality in a world that seemed, to many, to be both radically and irrevocably altered, dance appeared to be symptomatic of a complex – and often intersectional – matrix of contemporary social anxieties, particularly including race, class, and gender. Britain, despite winning the war, was also starting to question its place in the world. Following the Constitution of the Irish Free State (1922), the cracks were beginning to appear in Britain's empire. At the same time that this tottering imperialist nation was forced to reconsider its position in the world, the continuing vogue for all things American (which had initially developed in the later nineteenth century) – fuelled first by ragtime and jazz and the arrival of new American dances, and then through American movies and the widespread cult followings of successive waves of American screen idols and music stars – suggested that a new world order might be on the horizon in the not too distance future. This prompted considerable concern in many parts of British society.

Racial Anxieties and the Creation of the 'English' Ballroom Style

Beginning in the decade before the First World War – when the cakewalk, rag music, and American dances, such as the Boston Glide and Turkey Trot – first arrived in Britain, many British dancing teachers considered the new imports with alarm, perceiving in them a threat to the old social order. This impelled some to view these dances (and the music which accompanied them) as dangerous, and to associate them with a threatening degree of over-sexualisation, obviously informed by crude racist stereotypes driven by the African American origins of the new dances and music. Over a period of more than thirty years, as Tim Cresswell has demonstrated, British dance teachers – particularly through their official body the Imperial Society of Teachers of Dance (hereafter the ISTD) – invested considerable efforts into appropriating these African American dances, standardising the steps, and creating whitewashed English versions.[23]

The ISTD was formed in 1904,[24] following a meeting of some 200 dance teachers at the Hotel Cecil in Covent Garden. The date of this meeting – a full decade before the outbreak of the First World War – affirms that concerns about

---

[23] Tim Cresswell, '"You Cannot Shake that Shimmie Here": Producing Mobility on the Dance Floor', *Cultural Geographies*, Vol. 13 (2006), 55–77. On the development of the 'English' ballroom style, see also, Allison Abra, *Dancing in the English Style: Consumption, Americanisation and National Identity in Britain, 1918-50* (Manchester: Manchester University Press, 2017).

[24] The ISTD is still in existence (retaining its original name); see www.istd.org/home/ (last accessed 9 June 2023).

the arrival of popular new dance genres from the United States were already well established by the turn of the twentieth century. At the time, dance teacher qualifications did not exist, and anybody could set themselves up as a dancing teaching. Cresswell has commented that:

> Dancing was a key ingredient of the social lives of fashionable society, and the teachers [...] were keen to keep their dances out of the hands and feet of people who were not of the 'right background' [...] it was agreed that teachers of dance needed an organisation to protect their interests and regulate teaching standards [...] The stated purpose of the new body [the ISTD] was the creation of a uniform method of teaching and the encouragement of the higher education of the teacher.[25]

In his autobiography, Malcolm Munro offers a particularly striking insight into the suspicions which the new dancing styles aroused in early twentieth-century Liverpool. He commented on the horror with which dance teachers reacted to the appearance of the Cakewalk (a dance genre widely believed to have originated in the plantations of the Southern United States) in the summer of 1903 thus:

> It [the Cakewalk] enjoyed an immediate and sweeping success. Of course it was promptly tabooed by the 'unco guid'.[26] Indeed, the opposition amounted almost to a pitched battle, and all the evils of the day were put down to the effect of this heinous importation. Practically every one of the established dance academies gave the Cakewalk the 'cold shoulder', and looking back it may be true to say that it was this half-hearted welcome of a newcomer by the teachers of the day that made the Cakewalk the first free-style dance to be seen in the ballroom. Dancers, who were not catered for by the dancing masters, soon started to pick up the Cakewalk for themselves from the various exhibitions which were featured at the variety theatres and music halls.[27]

Munro's first-hand recollections here demonstrate the racist early twentieth-century trend to attribute a wide range of social vices to imported African American popular dances.

Debates about the new 'freakish', 'decadent', and 'romping' (to use the language of the time) steps and dances crystallised in the years following the First World War, at the same time that the popularity of new, jazz-influenced, styles of popular music became more entrenched. Contemporary press

---

[25] Cresswell, 'You Cannot Shake That Shimmie Here', 64. The ISTD was officially founded on 25 July 1904.
[26] 'Unco guid' is a Scottish term for a person who professes themselves to hold strict moral and religious standards. It is derived from the title of Robert Burns' *Address to the Unco Guid, or the Rigidly Righteous* (1786). Munro was no doubt influenced in his choice of this expression by his love of all things Scottish.
[27] Malcolm Munro, *Dancing Mad: An Autobiographical Dancing Diary* (unpublished, c1968), 28. All quotations used with permission of the Hamer-Munro family.

discourse reveals that both forms of popular culture were considered to have a prurient significance and were identified as potentially dangerous and threatening social influences. Largely in response to this, a Ballroom Branch of the ISTD was formed in 1924. Over the following decade and a half, the Ballroom Branch of the ISTD invested considerable efforts into taming and domesticating a whole range of new dances, nearly all of which had originated in the United States.

The ballroom dancer and musician Victor Silvester (1900–1978) had a vital input into this 'domestification' process. He was one of the founding members of the Ballroom Branch of the ISTD and subsequently served as its president from 1945 to 1958. True to the ISTD's initial aim of training dance teachers in the 'correct' steps, the Ballroom Branch quickly turned its attention to creating officially sanctioned – toned down – versions of the new dances, which teachers of ballroom dancing were then trained to pass on to the huge numbers of amateur ballroom dancers throughout the UK. This laid the foundations for (what is still referred to as) the 'English' style of ballroom dancing. Writing in 1968 in *Come Dancing* (a practical guide to ballroom dancing that was published as a tie-in to the BBC's popular and long-running ballroom dancing television programme of the same name),[28] Frank and Peggy Spencer observed that 'we teachers owe him [Silvester] debts […] he was a member of the Committee which tabulated the basic requirements for admission to membership of the Ballroom Branch of the ISTD, and continued to work on the analysing and standardizing of ballroom technique'.[29]

Silvester was also instrumental in taming the music that went with the dances, through his development of strict-tempo interpretations of popular dances. The initial impetus for this came from yet another meeting of dance teachers, this time held on 14 July 1929 at the Queen's Hotel in Leicester Square. At this conference, as Cresswell notes, it was 'agreed that the standardization of dances needed to make them as simple as possible, and that part of that simplification process was the designation of suitable speeds for each dance'.[30] In this instance, the dance teachers were acting in response to the tendency of different dance bands to play the same dances at very varied speeds, and also to pull the dances around by improvising (often inspired by the musicians' interest in jazz). As it proved difficult for the ISTD to police their officially condoned tempos,

---

[28] *Come Dancing* was first aired in 1950. It became one of the longest-running television shows of all time, as it continued (off and on) until 1998. It was relaunched in its current celebrity guise, as *Strictly Come Dancing* (thus merging the original title with that of Baz Luhrmann's 1992 film, *Strictly Ballroom*) in 2004.

[29] Frank and Peggy Spencer, *Come Dancing* (London: WH Allen, 1968), 16.

[30] Cresswell, 'You Cannot Shake that Shimmie Here', 67.

from 1935 onwards Silvester and his dance band began to issue commercial recordings of dance music in what he termed 'strict tempo'.[31] Commenting on how important Silvester's development of strict tempo was for dancers, Frank and Peggy Spencer have claimed that:

> […] his work as a committee member […] is not the only reason we teachers are grateful to him. In 1934 he formed a dance band to play dance music to 'strict tempo', and this was an enormous help […] what a blessing it was to be able to put on a Victor Silvester recording of a Foxtrot and be confident that the dance would be played at the correct speed. Dancers these days can have no idea how the pace of dances varied from band to band. The Foxtrot could be played at anything from forty to fifty bars a minute, and it is easy to guess how styles had to be rapidly altered according to who was conducting the band! But once Victor Silvester's band began recording, the problem was solved.[32]

Cresswell views the emergence of strict tempo as further evidence of the ISTD's drive to domesticate imported African American culture; commenting that 'Silvester's strict-tempo music stood in stark contrast to jazz music. Just as the ISTD ballroom dancing code had emerged in opposition to African American dance, so strict tempo was opposed to jazz'.[33]

Catherine Tackley has also noted the tendency of the contemporary press effectively to whitewash jazz; noting that its Black origins were 'generally only mentioned in contemporary articles to criticise'.[34] Viewed in this light, the ambitions of the ISTD to create an 'English' style can appear a sinister project of cultural misappropriation and hegemony. This can be viewed as an effort of cultural imperialism at a time when Britain's actual colonial power was beginning to falter.

The BBC was also actively complicit in the creation of a 'domesticated' version of popular music, suitable as edifying entertainment for the British public; as Tackley observes, the BBC initially had a somewhat 'sniffy' attitude towards all jazz and popular music.[35] She further notes that the word 'jazz', due to its 'undesirable associations' – that is negative racist stereotypes connected to African American culture – was not used in the BBC's programming schedules; rather they privileged the term 'dance music'.[36] She explains:

---

[31] Examples of Victor Silvester's 'strict tempo' recordings are available online; see, for example: STRICTLY BALLROOM (Various) – Victor Silvester and his Ballroom Orchestra – EMI Axis 8140962 – YouTube (last accessed 29 October 2024). To hear the contrast with 'hot' jazz, listen to, for example, Louis Armstrong's recordings with his Hot Five.
[32] Frank and Peggy Spencer, *Come Dancing*, 16–17.
[33] Cresswell, 'You Cannot Shake That Shimmie Here', 69.
[34] Parsonage, *The Evolution of Jazz in Britain*, 28.
[35] *Ibid.*, 45. The BBC was formed under Sir John Reith in 1923 with a mandate to provide radio as education for the masses.
[36] *Ibid.*

Although dance music was mere 'entertainment', it was still made to fit within the BBC's brief of providing material considered 'suitable' for the public. Dance music was considered acceptable entertainment as it was firmly associated with the respectable upper-class venues from which it was broadcast and, after all, was not meant to be listened to seriously but was considered to be purely functional for dancing.[37]

The BBC kept a very tight control over the 'quality'-cum-style of the bands which they transmitted; typically broadcasting those which performed at luxury London hotels, particularly the Savoy, and the BBC's own Dance Orchestra.[38] Once regional broadcasting became more established in the 1930s, the Grafton Rooms house band made live broadcasts on BBC North directly from Liverpool, thus affirming their acknowledged BBC 'quality'.

Class Anxieties

It was not only racial anxieties which the widespread popularity of dance in interwar Britain stimulated; dance's cross-class appeal also stirred up powerful class anxieties. Prior to the interwar period, ballroom dancing – as suggested by its very name – had been firmly the preserve of the upper and middle classes. The establishment of dance halls and palais de danse on a mass scale after the First World War opened up ballroom dancing to the working classes, who embraced the new trend with enthusiasm.[39] Reacting to what they perceived as a threat to their long-held privileged position by the rise in popularity of dance amongst the working classes partially motivated the ISTD's desire to, as Cresswell puts it in the quote earlier, 'keep their dances out of the hands and feet of people who were not of the "right background"'.[40] Despite their successes in codifying the new dances into their approved 'English' style and certifying dance teachers nationwide to teach their officially sanctioned versions of the dances, the ISTD utterly failed to keep ballroom dancing out of the feet of the working classes. As Rishona Zimring has observed, 'Dancing's social geography was inclusive, since dancing was a common pursuit among all classes owing to the democratization of leisure involved in the decrease in average weekly working hours and the falling cost of living.'[41] One example of such democratisation on Merseyside might be the growth of dance halls in what could be considered working-class districts. For instance, the Grafton Rooms

---

[37] *Ibid.*, 46.
[38] The BBC Dance Orchestra was formed in 1928. It was initially under the leadership of Jack Payne, until Henry Hall took over in 1932.
[39] For a detailed study of the development of dance halls throughout the UK during the interwar period, see Nott, *Going to the Palais*.
[40] Cresswell, 'You Cannot Shake That Shimmie Here', 64.
[41] Zimring, *Social Dance and the Modernist Imagination in Interwar Britain*, 39.

were based in Low Hill – an impoverished area of Liverpool during the interwar years. We might also cite various palais de danse along Scotland Road in Everton together with the (Munro managed) palais de danse in Bootle constructed in increasingly deprived districts. It should be noted that during Liverpool's 'dancing years', much of North Liverpool was already in decline; this was not necessarily the case in parts of South Liverpool. Nott has even claimed that although dancing had a 'cross-class appeal [...] by the mid-1920s it was pre-dominantly a working- and lower-middle-class activity'.[42] He further notes that 'representing its transition from an upper-middle-class pastime to one with a mass market [the most] regular dancing public was found to be young, predominantly female, and largely working class'.[43] The low price of admission to dance halls (which typically ranged from 6*d*. up to 2/6) facilitated dancing's popularity among the working class.[44]

Dance culture removed two of the visual markers of class: venue and dress. Nott has commented that dance halls were

> designed to create an atmosphere of glamour [...] most dance halls were similarly designed with a main dance floor, usually sprung and constructed of maple or oak, around which were placed clothed tables and chairs together with a band on a raised dais. The larger halls also had balconies where people could watch the dancing, together with cafés and restaurants, lounges, bars, and revolving bandstands.[45]

Everything combined to create the sense of luxury, elegance, and sophistication that had previously been restricted to the wealthy. The Grafton Rooms, which boasted the unique distinction – in Liverpool – of an oak sprung dance floor, exemplified this contemporary trend for luxuriance (see Figure 1). In an article dedicated to covering the grand opening of the Grafton Rooms on 9 February 1924 (almost four years before Malcolm Munro took over as manager), the *Liverpool Echo* described it thus:

> When you enter the spacious entrance hall, a short flight of steps gives you a clear view over the band, so the whole floor can be seen at once. A further few steps leads to the well-appointed café after the maze of syncopated dance. The oak floor is remarkably well sprung, and once its newness wears off it should become an ideal dance floor. The dance room has a bow ceiling, from which really fine decorative shaded lights are suspended, and one notices with pleasure the admirable arrangements of ventilation, an important point in connection with dancing. Round the open dance floor, which after the best

---

[42] Nott, *Music for the People*, 177.   [43] *Ibid.*, 177.
[44] Despite the Depression, working people in their late teens were actually one of the demographics with the largest amount of disposable income during the 1930s.
[45] Nott, *Music for the People*, 169.

Figure 1 The Interior of the Grafton Rooms (1932). Courtesy of Liverpool Central Library and Archives.

modern principles, is sunk slightly, there is a balcony where several hundred people may take refreshments or sit watching the gay scenes of the dance, while at the further end a spacious refreshment room and café is placed. The decorations of the new building are carried out in admirable taste, dark oak, white and cream being the prevailing colours, and these admirably show up the variegated colours of the magnificent lamp shades.[46]

Likewise, clothes, which prior to the First World War had been an immediate signifier of a person's social class, became much less so during the interwar period. Commenting on the importance of having a good set of clothes to go dancing in in 1930's Liverpool, Jenkins has observed that 'having a "good" dress to wear to the dance was vitally important for the female dancers. Looking good was very important and there were shops [in Liverpool] which sold and exchanged second-hand dresses'.[47] As Nott has commented, 'with the advent of mass produced clothing in the interwar period it became harder to distinguish class on the basis of clothing'.[48] Observing this difficulty of immediately identifying the class from which the clientele of the Grafton Rooms was

---

[46] Anonymous, 'Liverpool's Biggest Dance Hall Opens: A Real Palais de Danse for Merseyside', *Liverpool Echo* (10 February 1924), n.p.

[47] Jenkins, *'Let's Go Dancing'*, 9.   [48] Nott, *Music for the People*, 172.

drawn, Munro mused (when he was interviewed as part of the Mass Observation project in 1939) that:

> It is hard to say what class people are in today. The girls work in Littlewoods, Vernons, and Ogden Pools. The boys are mainly in shops. They are not labouring workers. They are what you may call the sedentary occupations – clerks, shop boys etc. There are not many labourers. They are too tired after a hard day's work.[49]

Women, in particular, were influenced by the fashions for hair and clothing originating in Hollywood and transmitted to Britain via the cinema. For perhaps the first time, working-class women were able to replicate (if only through one set of 'best' clothes) the styles of the rich and famous.

Anxieties of Gender and Sexuality

As noted earlier, single young women made up the largest demographic who regularly went dancing in interwar Britain. This meant that the dance hall also became a site in which widely felt gender anxieties were played out. As Zimring expresses it:

> The sense of rupture created by the war involved a crisis in gender relations; war emasculated the nation […] and the female body became central […] to the maintenance of the nation: women became the redemptive embodiment of the nation's civilizing values, which would explain why the spectacle of women dancing in public could assuage anxiety, by symbolizing the vitality of healthy female bodies, but also exacerbate it, by exhibiting them on the loose.[50]

Many contemporary commentators were concerned about what they perceived as wide-spread gender confusion, especially among young women; concerns which were exacerbated by the falling birth rate and the new 1920's female fashions for dropped waists and bobbed hair, which created an androgynous look. Dancing in fact allowed the new women's fashions – symbolised by the iconic 'flapper' look: raised hemline, dropped waist, beads, bobbed hair, make-up, perfume, and cloche hat – to be shown off to full advantage. As Tackley notes, well-known exhibition dancers of the day, such as Irene Castle (one of the first women to sport bobbed hair), became important trend-setters. Tackley has even gone so far as to claim that the development of the new dancing styles after the First World War are attributable to the increased social and sexual freedoms of women. She argues that the war had brought women into greater contact with

---

[49] M-O A: MDJ: 5/F, A. H., 'Manager Grafton Rooms Liverpool', 18 May 1939, 2; cited from Nott, *Music for the People*, 179.

[50] Zimring, *Social Dance and the Modernist Imagination in Interwar Britain*, 13.

men, whilst the *carpe diem* philosophy of the war continued to influence the increasingly liberalised sexual mores of the interwar period.[51] As the new dances required close physical contact, Tackley goes so far as to claim that dance halls themselves 'symbolised women's greater social emancipation'.[52]

Whilst this view that the First World War brought about great social and sexual emancipation for women is widely held – and is undeniably partly true – the reality of the situation was somewhat more complex. Although the Representation of the People Act granted the vote to women of property over the age of thirty in 1918; this was not extended to all women until a decade later in 1928. Prior to 1928, as Zimring has commented:

> Debate about the 'flapper vote' flourished,[53] and the postwar period saw a widespread preoccupation with the female as androgyne, sexless but libidinous, infantile but precocious, self-sufficient but demographically, economically and socially superfluous. The flapper was an emblem of modernity even as she embodied ancient stereotypes of dangerous femininity. With the anxiety about flappers came a discourse about the conspicuous and ambiguous sexuality of adult women.[54]

Instead of viewing the period immediately following the First World War as marking tremendous advancements for women's liberation – crowned by the granting of suffrage and greater access to employment – it might be more useful to view these years as offering women a circumscribed degree of greater freedom.

As the vote for all women was won only slowly, women's employment throughout the interwar period was also a complex issue. Although women's work had been essential during the war, it had always been strongly emphasised at the time that women's war work was only ever intended to be an exceptional temporary measure, made necessary purely by wartime conditions. The government, whose priority was to provide employment for returning veterans, acted to remove women from their wartime occupations through the Restoration of Pre-War Practices Act (1919), which forced the majority of women out of their wartime jobs, as soon as the war was over. As Martin Pugh has noted, many local authorities also operated marriage bars, which meant that they 'simply sacked female employees, notably teachers, nurses, doctors and cleaners, as soon as they married'.[55] The view frequently advanced at the time – and also during the Depression of the 1930s – that women were taking up men's jobs

---

[51] Parsonage, *The Evolution of Jazz in Britain*, 41.   [52] Ibid.
[53] The 1929 general election – the first in which all women over 21 were eligible to vote – was even dubbed the 'flapper election'.
[54] Zimring, *Social Dance and the Modernist Imagination in Interwar Britain*, 13.
[55] Martin Pugh, *'We Danced All Night': A Social History of Britain between the Wars* (London: Bodley Head, 2008), 182.

was an oversimplification. By the interwar period, whole sectors of the workforce had become sexually diversified; secretaries and switchboard operators were nearly all women, for example, whilst demand for female servants increased. Such crude (and somewhat emotive) arguments also ignored the economic reality that many young husbands had returned from the First World War disabled and/or shell-shocked, meaning that their wives had to become the main breadwinners. Similar situations also occurred throughout the Depression, when many men faced long-term unemployment.

If the figure of the young, single woman dancing as a pastime aroused social anxieties during the interwar period, then the figure of the professional female dancer did even more so. Beyond the famous women ballroom dancers of the period, such as Irene Castle and Josephine Bradley, the professional dancers employed by many dance halls – known as exhibition dancers – were often viewed with suspicion.[56] These dancers were commonly stigmatised as having relaxed sexual morals by a society in which pre- and extra-marital sex (although common) remained taboo.[57] Although, as in earlier periods, female musicians did not tend to be regarded with as much moral suspicion as female dancers, they could also find their reputations compromised by their occupations.[58] Despite this, women band musicians existed in large numbers during the interwar period. As positions for women within otherwise all-male bands tended to be restricted to singers, female instrumentalists often formed their own all-women bands, as discussed in greater detail in Section 5. Mary Hamer provides a fascinating case study of how a woman – and one from a working-class, Irish Catholic background – could confront the contemporary gender anxieties not only of a woman working professionally as both a dancer and a musician, but also directly challenge the concerns of the day regarding a woman's true place in society by directing an otherwise all-male band; literally inverting the patriarchy.

3 Dancers, Musicians, and Managers: Creating Mr Malcolm Munro, Marie Daly, and Wilf Hamer

Mary Hamer was born Mary Daly in Wallasey, a small Merseyside town close to Liverpool, in 1904, and brought up in 8 Beatrice Street, in what was then a very

---

[56] The ambiguous social positions held by professional dancers is alluded to in several novels of the period, including Dorothy L. Sayer's 1932 Lord Peter Wimsey crime novel *Have His Carcase* and Agatha Christie's 1942 Miss Marple mystery, *The Body in the Library*, in both of which the murder victims are exhibition ballroom dancers.

[57] Thus, the centuries-old prejudice of associating professional female dancers with loose sexual morals or even prostitution continued unabated throughout the interwar period.

[58] For an overview of women in British popular music during the earlier twentieth century, see Catherine Parsonage and Kathy Dyson, 'The History of Women in Jazz in Britain', in Patricia Adkins Chiti (ed.), *Women in Jazz/Donne in Jazz* (Rome: Editore Columbo, 2007), 129–140.

impoverished area. One of thirteen children, she came from a large Irish Catholic immigrant family. Her mother was a seamstress, and her father imported dairy products. Although she attended St Joseph's Catholic Primary School in Seacombe and dancing lessons at Killen's Dance School in Wallasey, she did not receive formal piano lessons. It appears that neither of her parents was especially musical, but that she taught herself to play the piano by ear and was never confident reading music.[59] She left school at thirteen and supported herself financially by playing the piano. By 1918 she was leading her first dance band – 'Mary Daly's Orchestra' – at the Co-operative Hall in Wallasey.[60]

Becoming a popular musician might appear an odd career choice for a young woman from a working-class, Catholic background, especially one whose family were not musicians. Driven by the contemporary craze for the new music and dances, the number of popular musicians increased dramatically in the earlier twentieth century; effectively creating a new form of employment. Many band musicians had little or no formal musical training. As Nott has commented, 'entry into the dance band scene was less rigid than into other parts of the music profession. This meant it was able to grow rapidly, attracting large numbers of people who would previously have had limited contact with music.'[61] The comparative cheapness of popular dance band instruments (such as trumpets or saxophones) and the relative ease with which these could be learned[62] enabled the number of dance band musicians to grow rapidly. By the early 1920s, as Nott has observed, 'the dance music profession [...] was sufficiently large to provide a source of live dance music in virtually every community in Britain'.[63]

In the early 1920s, Mary Daly became acquainted with the Liverpool-based ballroom dancer, dancing teacher, and manager, John Murphy (Malcolm Munro).[64] This meeting proved to be a turning point in both their careers, as over the ensuing decades they drew on each other's complimentary skills to shape much of Liverpool's popular music and dance culture. In the following section, the early careers of both are considered, with particular attention paid to their time working at the Embassy Rooms, where Daly was not only employed as a professional exhibition ballroom dancer but also led the renowned house band, the Embassy Bohemians. Her early career demonstrates that she was

---

[59] We are grateful to George Hamer for information regarding Mary Hamer's family background.
[60] Munro, *Dancing Mad*, 74.   [61] Nott, *Music for the People*, 136.
[62] Many music publishers produced tutors to cater for this burgeoning market of new players. *Melody Maker*, for instance, issued regular instrumental courses written by prominent professional dance band musicians.
[63] Nott, *Music for the People*, 128.
[64] For the remainder of this section, Murphy/Munro is referred to by his family name Murphy until discussion turns to his career following his decision to adopt the professional name Malcolm Munro in January 1923. Thereafter, he is referred to as Munro. All references to his autobiography credit him as Munro throughout, however, as this is the name that he intended to publish it under.

already a well-established musician and dancer within Liverpool's dance music scene, and one who clearly saw herself as a leader, by the mid-1920s.

John Murphy

Malcolm Munro was born John Murphy in 1887. Like Daly he also came from a large Irish Catholic immigrant family, though one that was considerably better off. The Murphys were based in Latimer Street in one of the traditional Irish Catholic districts of Everton, in Liverpool, where Mr Murphy senior owned a bakery. Murphy was one of twelve children and second eldest. His young friends included two brothers: Leo and Tommy Montgomery. Their father owned the Westminster Music Hall and also ran the Rotunda Theatre. In his autobiography Murphy claimed that:

> It is from that association at such an early age that I date the beginning of my infatuation with show business. They took me to the 'Wessie' as it was called, one night every week, and I well remember their mother, a very charming and grand dame, taking the money at the pit pay box; although we of course never paid, being included in that well known category of 'dead heads' or non-paying patrons.[65]

Murphy was determined to pursue this childhood 'infatuation', learning to dance and becoming a professional exhibition ballroom dancer and dancing teacher. Prior to the First World War he was employed as a dancing instructor by several of Liverpool's dance academies, including those run by the Clarke and Cheshire families, which were both well established by the early twentieth century.[66]

John Murphy and Liverpool's First World War Dance Music Craze

Murphy enlisted in the army in November 1915, and served with the Liverpool Scottish Regiment for the remainder of the First World War.[67] In his autobiography, he reminisced that returning home for ten days of leave from active service in January 1918 he found Liverpool's popular entertainment scene in full swing:

> Mrs Clarke's academy was going strong, and she was also running assemblies in Belmont Hall. The crowds were dancing the 'Gaby-Trot', which was the British Association Foxtrot of 1916 to the tune of 'Hor D'oeuvres' and the 'Maxina' which was the prize dance of 1917, invented by the Hurndalls, who netted about £10,000 in royalties, so amazingly did the public take to this

---

[65] Munro, *Dancing Mad*, 5.
[66] Mrs Clarke's dancing academy was situated at Carisbrooke Road, Walton (L5) and Mrs Chesire's dancing academy was based in Great George Street in the city centre.
[67] Munro, *Dancing Mad*, 46.

sequence dance. Sequence dancing, still very popular, was soon to give way to non-sequence dancing and jazz. I found time, too, to visit Mrs Cheshire at her ballroom in Great George Street. She was running there a new set dance called 'Roulette', which was very much like a 'lancers' but set to modern dance figures: waltz, foxtrot, two-step, one-step, tango.[68]

When Murphy once again returned to Liverpool following the Armistice, he recollected that as soon as he had stepped back onto Liverpool soil, he noticed that:

> [...] the dance halls and academies were packed. At Belmont Hall, Mr and Mrs Clarke were showing the 'Jazz Roll' which had evolved from the previous year's 'Hawai'ian Jazz', and for the first time in the North, the 'Victor Waltz'; the British Association Prize dance of 1918 was presented by Edith Clarke and myself.
> We attended a Victory Ball at the Philharmonic Hall [...] This was one occasion when to my mind there were far too many banjos and trombones. [...] together with a drummer who sounded as if he were banging a lot of kitchen utensils which I saw hanging over his outfit, struck me as unnecessarily noisy, especially as I had just come back from a surfeit of noise 'over there'.[69]

This statement is persuasive evidence that Murphy encountered an early jazz dance band in the city. He observed that it 'was the new jazz style that was creeping in[to] the non-sequence dancing',[70] perhaps suggesting that it was rather unstructured, allowing dancers to be somewhat unabandoned. His comments also suggest that he thought the band to be a noisy aggregation – particularly the percussionist – and somewhat grudgingly groaned that he had already experienced more than enough noise in France. Personal tastes aside, one thing is certain from these comments: for Murphy, a dancer brought up in the 'old school' of European dance, the very tenor of popular dance music was beginning to change: syncopation was beginning to dominate. (Thus, his initial concerns were not dissimilar to other contemporary British dancers, as discussed in Section 2.) It perhaps also bears witness to the fact that Black and Black-inspired sounds were changing British popular music and dance. We do not know whether Murphy encountered any African American units in France during that final year of the war. However, we might speculate that the raucous jazz band he encountered in Liverpool perhaps came as something of an unwelcome surprise. It should also be acknowledged that he was well known in dance circles in Liverpool and was warmly welcomed back to the fold by those with whom he had previously worked. Therefore, we feel that he might have been something of a traditionalist; his comments may have also harked

---

[68] *Ibid.*, 61.   [69] *Ibid.*, 73.   [70] *Ibid.*, 74.

back to a local dance scene which perhaps represented for him somewhat happier times prior to the outbreak of war in 1914.

While on his final leave from army service, Murphy attended as many venues and ballrooms as he was able, thereby awarding us a litany of Liverpool-based entertainment locations from the immediate post–First World War period. Aside from visiting the Philharmonic Hall on this return visit, he also mentions Daulby Hall ('packed with Americans'), Great George Street Assembly Rooms, the Hippodrome, and the Olympia. He informs us that at St Martin's Hall, the Holyoake Hall and Walton Hall (the latter two being well known Co-operative Society halls), the Baths, The Yemen Café (Bold Street), and Stanley Hall, Bootle: 'jazz bands were all the go.'[71] He also cites a few jazz bands for us:

> We had Sam Bonner's, Mrs. Rutherford's, Alex and Mac's, Aggie O'Neill's, Jack Llewellyn's, Jack and Jimmie Leight's and Davies and Sharp's with Arthur Davies at the Adelphi Hotel. Johnnie Cotton's Harmony Four, Collin's Red Orchestra which played mainly for society functions, and Mary Daly's Orchestra […] in Wallasey.[72]

That Daly's orchestra is namechecked is of particular interest to us, as it affirms both that Murphy initially encountered her in the period immediately following the First World War and that he found her band as worthy of a mention (despite her young age) as any of the others. (It is also noteworthy that two other bands being led by women are mentioned: Mrs Rutherford's and Aggie O'Neill's.)

The Post-War Dancing Master

Murphy was finally demobbed in February 1919, and once permanently back in Liverpool, he soon discovered that a new generation of dancers and dance tutors had replaced many of the older instructors. He informs us a little begrudgingly that by this time 'Jazz and Yankee dancing was the vogue'.[73] However, he was able to re-join Clarke's Dancing Academy as a freelance dance instructor. Income from such work would have been entirely reliant upon the popularity of the academy for whom one danced and the willingness of learners to provide tips for their professional partners. In his autobiography Munro confesses that it took him twelve months to get over his army service years and admits that, although happy to be home, he also at times felt extremely lonely and missed the comradeship of his army pals. However, once this feeling had finally evaporated to at least a manageable level, he was urged by the growing coterie of young people he was teaching as a freelancer, to take up professional ballroom dancing

---

[71] *Ibid.* [72] *Ibid.* [73] *Ibid.*, 76.

in a full-time capacity. This meant taking examinations with the NATD (National Association of Teachers of Dancing):[74]

> I was keenly interested in the technical side of dancing, began to teach privately, and secured a goodly number of clients. Mrs Cheshire prepared me for the examination for membership of the National Association of Teachers of Dancing and, a little later on, the British Association. With the help of the family and some friends, I rented the Gordon Institute on Monday evenings for assemblies,[75] and Wednesday afternoons for classes for the season 1920-21 commencing in September [...] The Monday evening enterprise was a great success and continued for a full season. The Wednesday afternoon was in the nature of an instruction class, and was very successful, eventually grew to the two hundred mark [...][76]

By the winter of 1921 Murphy was also playing piano for a dance teacher colleague, Jack Ellis, at Walton Church Parish Hall. After a short period of time, Murphy was somewhat unceremoniously sacked by Ellis because he (Ellis) wanted a pianist who could 'thump it out'. Murphy suggests that his own playing might have been a little too refined for Ellis at this stage.[77] This might provide further evidence that jazz was 'all the rage', with Murphy perhaps less inclined to play syncopated accompaniments.

The Bootle Palais de Danse

However, ever the entrepreneur, Murphy then arranged a 'London Club Night' at the same venue and also became the promoter of a small, syncopated band. On the dancefloor he taught the 'Spanish Vogue' dance, which, according to his autobiography, was the very first attempt to popularise Latin American dancing in Liverpool. All such activities, plus playing for private functions, promoting dances, and his now officially 'affiliated' NATD classes, led to him being offered in March 1922 the manager's position at a new Palais de Danse on Knowsley Road, Bootle.[78] As he reminisced in his autobiography:

---

[74] Founded in 1906, the NATD (like the ISTD, discussed in Section 2) also offered dancing qualifications.
[75] The Gordon Institute was located on Stanley Road on the Liverpool-Bootle borders. The Institute was opened in 1886 and was reputed to be Britain's oldest boys club. It was built at a cost of £50,000 by a William Cliff, a Liverpool merchant, as a memorial to his eldest son who died aged 11 in 1853. The Institute was so named to commemorate and perpetuate the memory of Maj. General Charles Gordon (Gordon of Khartoum). More recently the building has housed the Kirkdale Community Centre.
[76] Munro, *Dancing Mad*, 77–78.   [77] *Ibid.*, 80.
[78] The Knowsley Road Palais de Dance had previously been a cinema named firstly the Picture Palace of Bootle and then in 1912 the Empire Picture Theatre. The building was initially constructed as the Bootle Institute in 1882.

'I received the munificent salary of £4 per week, with the use of the ballroom for private lessons and classes.'[79]

The Bootle Palais de Danse – which first opened its doors on Easter Monday 1922 – proved to be an immediate success, for the dance craze was growing exponentially. In fact (and perhaps owing to Murphy's NATD qualifications and contacts), the venue appears to have become a true centre of excellence for ballroom dancing, attracting not only Merseyside's best dancers, but also highly regarded dancing adjudicators from across the Northwest of England. They would advise on the steps and movements of specific dances to illustrate how leading amateur competition dancers (such as Murphy) might 'do it' under the auspices of the NATD.

Mary Daly Partners John Murphy

By the early 1920s, Mary Daly had become John Murphy's professional dance partner and pianist. They competed together for the first time in May 1922, when they won second place at the Blackpool Dance Festival for the 'Chinn Chinn'.[80] By this time, Daly was leading her own small band at the Bootle Palais de Danse, where Murphy had been appointed manager. He hired her as both resident pianist around whom a small band was assembled *and* as an exhibition ballroom dancer. Daly frequently partnered Murphy at the venue, exhibiting various dances; the couple also took part in several prominent competitive dancing events across the Northwest. Murphy later recalled that the Bootle Palais de Danse was extremely well patronised by locals, and that the venue was reviewed in the *Liverpool Evening Express* as being 'a cosy little ballroom with soft lighting and a beautiful springy maple floor, with an assembly of smartly dressed young ladies and gentlemen dancing in the modern style, and a young gentleman M.C. who possessed the "heaven sent gift of tact"'.[81] We presume that Murphy's teaching methods together with his dance partnership with Daly greatly assisted new dancers to develop their skills on the dancefloor. The Bootle Palais de Danse ensemble also included Murphy's much younger brother Wilf on banjo. Wilf Murphy (professionally known as Wilf Hamer) was twenty years younger than John, having been born in 1907. In an interview given to BBC Radio Merseyside in the 1980s, Daly recalled Wilf, as 'a young lad who arrived in short trousers in order to be in the band'.[82]

---

[79] Munro, *Dancing Mad*, 81.   [80] *Ibid.*, 82–83.   [81] *Ibid.*, 85.
[82] Mary Hamer, Interview with BBC Radio Merseyside (1980s); cited from Jenkins, *'Let's Go Dancing'*, 39.

Move to the Embassy Rooms

In 1923, Murphy applied for the position of MD ('Maitre de Danse') at the soon-to-be-opened Embassy Rooms; an up-market venue in Mount Pleasant, Liverpool, previously known as the Wellington Rooms.[83] This establishment was managed by a consortium led by Alderman Edwin Haigh, a local self-made man who had also opened billiard halls and cinemas across the city. Although a popular venue amongst certain echelons of Liverpool society, the syndicate had been unable to make enough money from the Wellington Rooms because under the terms of its existing licence it was only allowed limited opening hours. Therefore, it was agreed in 1922 by the directors of the venue to establish and incorporate a limited company so that the premises could be purchased outright and re-opened as a public ballroom (rather than its previous rather 'exclusive' designation), thus relaxing licencing restrictions. Given his evident knowledge of the local entertainment industry Haigh was also appointed managing director.

Interviews for a new manager/MD of the re-named Embassy Rooms commenced in January 1923 and impressed with John Murphy, Haigh offered him the job. We do not know whether there was competition for this position or whether Murphy was 'invited' to apply for the job; after all, his reputation had grown exponentially at the Bootle Palais de Danse. Upon Murphy's acceptance of the offer Haigh then suggested that his new employee should adopt a 'professional name'. Various reasons for this have been suggested to us, including (from the family) the contemporary discrimination against the Irish Catholic community. Perhaps the Irish connotations attached to the 'Murphy' surname did signify something 'undesirable' for Haigh. However, to somewhat counter this interpretation, in his autobiography Murphy/Munro explained this name change thus:

> As it was usual in show business, I agreed with him that it would be a good idea. A *Dancing Times* lay on his desk, and with his secretary we went through the names in the advertising columns. Eventually we evolved a name and John Murphy became Malcolm Munro, the Malcolm being taken from the Malcolm Ives Orchestra and the Munro from the MacMunro Orchestras […] It was then arranged that in all publicity matters my new name was to appear as 'Malcolm Munro, Maitre De Danse'.[84]

---

[83] The neo-classical building was designed by renowned architect Edmund Aikin (1780–1820) and was constructed between 1815 and 1816 as a subscription assembly room for the very exclusive 'Wellington Club'. It was in constant use by Liverpool's high society for assemblies, dance balls, and parties.

[84] Munro, *Dancing Mad*, 88–89.

Figure 2 Malcolm Munro in 1927. Courtesy of Liverpool Central Library and Archives.

Thus, the well-known moniker of 'Malcolm Munro' materialised.[85] Figure 2 reproduces a publicity image of Munro produced just a few years later (in 1927), when he had firmly settled into his 'Malcolm Munro' persona.

It seems that prior to Munro's appointment, Haigh had already engaged an orchestra via the renowned Liverpool Sharp and Davies agency. Harry Sharp and Arthur Davies were not only well-known locally based musical agents, but also accomplished musicians (Sharp trombone, Davies piano and bandleader) and they ran their own band. It was this ensemble that had been booked into the Embassy Rooms by Haigh. The Sharp and Davies band consisted of twelve musicians, including a certain Gerald Bright, later known as the celebrated band leader, 'Geraldo'.[86] However, Munro also wished to employ what he later described as a small relief band of four. This unit would effectively be used as a reserve, one which might be called upon to play when larger bands had not been booked, or not turned up, and/or to play during intervals. It was common practice for ballrooms and restaurants to employ small combos consisting of versatile musicians who might be employed at reduced rates. The members of this diminutive combination comprised at least two members of the Bootle

---

[85] The Scottish sound may also have been a conscious tribute to his love of all things associated with Scotland.

[86] Geraldo (1904–1974) was one of the most well-known British dance band leaders of the 1930s.

Palais de Danse band: pianist-leader Mary Daly and banjoist Wilf Hamer,[87] plus percussionist Jack Cheshire and violinist Harold Ormian.

The Embassy Rooms duly opened on Monday, 29 January 1923, and was an immediate success. According to Munro:

> Anybody who was anybody in Liverpool society was there. The night was a brilliant success and congratulations were showered on me from every angle [...] Mr Haigh appeared resplendent in his tails, probably the first tail suit he had ever worn [and] went round playing 'old-harry' with the staff generally.[88]

The 'modern foxtrot' was presented by Munro and Topsy Steele (another of his professional dancing partners) that evening, whilst the star attractions were two renowned exhibition dancers, Cynthia and Cyril Horrocks, who usually danced at the Belgravia Hotel in London. The following afternoon the Horrocks also gave a lecture-demonstration to a large gathering of Merseyside dancing teachers. Much later, Daly was to recall of her days at the Embassy:

> When I wasn't playing solo piano on the other side of the ballroom, I used to dance the rest of the evening. I always got the solo spot because that was the feature and I always liked that. They would put the Limelight on and darken the ballroom and people would get a bit romantic and loved to dance to these waltzes.[89]

There is something especially atmospheric about these albeit later comments. The romantic nature of the environment, the lighting via the Limelight in the darkened ballroom, and the use of the waltz as a romantic 'go to' dance all indicate discrete, yet authentic, bodily contact. The use of the waltz was, of course, vital in creating such an atmosphere. During an era in which new dance crazes were being invented almost at will, the European waltz was still holding sway as the premier contact dance.[90] It was not 'lewd' (to use terminology from the 1920s) but instead rather 'classically sophisticated', with partners held closely as the pair moved in a conjoined rotary motion. Such was its enduring popularity that by 1923 the waltz had even been simplified with a step-together-step ('valse à deux temps') so that practically

---

[87] In taking the professional name Hamer, we believe that Wilf was most likely influenced by a middle Murphy brother: William, who died in March 1916. William Murphy, who had also been a popular musician, had used the professional name Will E. Hamer. Hamer was also the family name of the Murphy brothers' paternal grandmother, Elizabeth.

[88] Munro, *Dancing Mad*, 91.   [89] Mary Hamer quoted in Jenkins, *'Let's Go* Dancing', 40–41.

[90] For an important study of the perseverance of the European waltz into the interwar period, see Theresa Buckland's two-part article, 'How the Waltz Was Won', *Dance Research: The Journal of the Society for Dance Research*, Vol. 36, No. 1 (Summer 2018), 1–32 and Vol. 36, No. 2 (Winter 2018), 138–172.

anyone could step to that three-time rhythm; also very easy, one suspects, for Daly to teach 'on the spot' in the Embassy Rooms.

It is certainly important to consider how, during that early-mid-1920s dance craze period, local orchestras such as those at the Embassy created levels of both excellence and relevance not hitherto attempted. Excellence because competition was stiff, bands were plentiful, and dance venues able to pick and choose; relevance because one had to play the appropriate dance music at the most apposite times during an evening's entertainment (and to audiences who wished to express themselves physically). An understanding of popular dance, not only via the long-established traditional waltz mentioned earlier, but also the foxtrot was in fact utterly essential.[91] Other dances might have come and gone during this time but both dance forms still hold sway to this day. To have a young championship-standard dancer such as Daly also calling the shots as a band*leader*, together with the assistance of her occasional dance partner Munro as manager/MD, must have been a huge financial advantage for the Embassy Rooms and it certainly helped create an atmosphere of not only excellence and relevance, but also sophistication.

The Embassy Bohemians

So popular at the Embassy Rooms was the small band of local musicians and dancers who, it seemed, could turn their hand to whichsoever dance or style happened to be the 'latest thing' (and indeed the aforementioned more traditional material), that the Embassy Rooms' management did not renew their contract with the Sharp and Davies Orchestra. For the forthcoming winter season 1923/24 they instead reformed the core of this smaller resident group into the venue's full-time outfit. The band was initially to consist of an all-male line-up comprising Gerald Bright (Geraldo, piano), Harold Ormian (violin), Alex Matthews (percussion), and Wilf Hamer (banjo). Like Alex Matthews, Gerald Bright had been a member of the Sharp and Davies Orchestra and had then served as Arthur Davies' pianist at the Blackpool Tower Ballroom. Bright had apparently gained something of a name for himself among dancers there; however, according to Munro, he wished to return to Liverpool.

Therefore, Munro's initial intentions were to 'feature' Bright as part of the Embassy house band and employ Mary Daly only as the venue's relief solo pianist and dancer. However, Bright's request of a salary of £10 per week was

---

[91] The foxtrot had been growing in popularity since around 1914, when Irene and Vernon Castle exhibited it in the United States. The dance was associated with the new jazz sounds and freer movements from the outset. The African American bandleader James Reese Europe was hired, alongside a handpicked eighteen-piece all African American band, to accompany the Castles' touring this exciting dance right across the United States. By the early 1920s, it was firmly entrenched as standard modern ballroom dance within the UK.

immediately turned down by Haigh and the young musician promptly left. Consequently, and one might suggest almost by default, Daly was asked to become the new pianist and hence *de facto* bandleader, but of course at only half Bright's demanded rate: £5 per week.[92] Historically, this was an interesting development that could be seen from at least two perspectives: one being that Munro was able to squeeze his sometime dancing partner into the Embassy Rooms' full-time payroll (rather than have her work as a 'go to' freelancer), but another being that women musicians were always far cheaper a commodity than their male counterparts (in this case, exactly half the rate demanded by Bright). Such demeaning financial differentials were, of course, common practice in the city of Liverpool where, at least by the turn of the century, the city's prosperity relied upon thousands of skilled and unskilled women working for menial wages.

The band was christened 'the Embassy Bohemians'; an excellent name to be sure. A saxophonist was also added to this new house band; this might have been to update both their sound and image via this important sonic style indicator (as far as we know Wilf Hamer played banjo at this stage). Therefore, Jacques Brown – later a highly regarded BBC radio producer – was recruited perhaps to help them embrace the 'jazz age'. Speaking in the 1980s to BBC Radio Merseyside's Clive Garner, Daly took direct credit for the appointment of Brown:

> There was a café there [the corner of Lord Street and Whitechapel in Liverpool's city centre] called the Edinburgh Café, and they had a tea dance underneath. The BBC studio [6LV] was above that. I was in Davis' Arcade [next door] buying music one day and the girl behind the counter said, 'that man plays saxophone'. So, I went to him, and I said, 'do you play the saxophone'? and he said 'well, I do but I don't'. So, I said 'what do you mean – you do but you don't? come up and give an audition at the Embassy Rooms', and he got the job if you don't mind! Afterwards he became a BBC producer, Jacques Brown.[93]

It is noteworthy that, here, Daly asserts to have made the first moves to employ Brown, for, in his autobiography, Munro claims that Brown simply walked into the Embassy Rooms one day looking for a gig ('he admitted that he could only play one tune but he said he would be able to play anything by the time we wanted him in September [...] Mr Brown must have created a good impression on our old man, Mr Haigh, who turned to me and with great enthusiasm declared "he's good Munro, he's got 'pathos', we'll book him".'[94]). However, according to Garner, Daly's initial approach to Brown at

---

[92] Munro, *Dancing Mad*, 100.   [93] Mary Hamer cited from Jenkins, *'Let's Go Dancing'*, 50.
[94] Munro, *Dancing Mad*, 100–101.

the Edinburgh Café was, for him, the most likely occurrence. Garner informed Mike Brocken that:

> Mary was a very hands-on individual – even when I got to know her in her later years, she was very pro-active. She had something about her. I bet she'd have been told by Munro to keep an eye out for a sax player and that's exactly what she would have done. Also, the Edinburgh Café and Davies' Arcade on the corner of Whitechapel and Lord Street were the places you would meet musicians looking for a gig. So, for me it was undoubtedly Mary who made that contact; Munro is probably telling the truth about Brown strolling into the Embassy, but for me that would have been after Mary's prompting.[95]

This informs us that, even at a young age, Daly regarded herself (as perhaps did Munro) as a truly professional bandleader and that she readily accepted the responsibilities of that role, especially being on the lookout for good musicians. This is thought-provoking when one considers this era of low wages for women workers, together with those married women who were simply not allowed to work at all.[96] Fellow female Liverpudlian musician Margaret Doyle later acknowledged the problems most women might have experienced as band members during those interwar years:

> There wouldn't be many women playing in those days. We also had Jessie Rives in the Follies [Margaret's band], she was only a youngster, she played the violin. She married Ian Ewing afterwards. He was a traveller in something. He also played the piano in the band. 'Cos I mean it wasn't your occupation, it was your relaxation more in those days.[97] It was different for me as I was with my husband you see, and he didn't like dancing. Once we went to the Holyoake [Hall in Wavertree, Liverpool]. We tried dancing only he'd got two left feet and I wasn't much better, but he liked playing and he liked doing something that I was doing too. Women didn't go out to work in those days. You spent your life just looking after your kids when they were little, not like nowadays. I know my mother-in-law thought I was terrible leaving them, because of the dancing. Mind, you didn't go out until about 8 o'clockish and the little ones were supposed to be in bed by then.[98]

Notwithstanding the comments of the semi-professional Margaret Doyle, it appears that Daly was already in the early stages of becoming openly recognised across Liverpool's burgeoning dance band scene as a highly skilled professional danceband leader, musician, and ballroom dancer. In her own way, Daly was

---

[95] Clive Garner to Mike Brocken (October 1997).
[96] Many women in Liverpool (as elsewhere) – including Brocken's own mother and maternal grandmother – once married, were not allowed by their husbands to go to work.
[97] Unlike the fully professional Mary Hamer, Margaret Doyle was one of the many semi-professional musicians active within Liverpool's interwar dance music scene.
[98] Margaret Doyle cited from Jenkins, 'Let's Go Dancing', 42–43.

helping bring about a little more respect and perhaps even artistic autonomy for women artists in Liverpool's growing popular music industry, and this could only have been a good thing while male musicians and dancers utterly dominated.

Presenting The Blues at the Embassy Rooms

The decision to add a saxophone player was also an interesting development for the band, associated as the instrument was by the early 1920s with early forms of jazz (even for some perhaps the blues?) and regarded by many as a rather 'sexy', syncopated instrument. We have already seen that by at least 1923 jazz syncopation was attracting the interest of dancers. Of course, long before the saxophone became a classic movie style indicator of love in the 'talkies', it was considered a sexualised instrument. As Stephen Cottrell affirms:

> The saxophone's close association with dance music and jazz in the first half of the twentieth century has been without question the single most important reason for its present widespread familiarity. But for much of the 1920s and 30s particularly, and for many years thereafter, the instrument suffered because of this. The arrival of these new styles was accompanied by an outraged response from the moral majority (as is so often the case in the development of Western popular music ...), who saw in them evidence of every kind of youthful dissolution. The opposition to what was construed as 'jazz' was especially fierce [...] And since the unfamiliar sound and shape of this relatively new instrument took a dominant role in many of the musical proceedings, it could clearly be identified as the principal miscreant, at whose door much of the blame for this decadent musical behaviour could be laid.[99]

Malcolm Munro describes an event that year at the Embassy Rooms when with 'piano leader' Daly, 'we were the first in the North of England to present the newest dance sensation: the Blues'.[100] We presume that Brown's sax playing featured in this presentation. It appears that a blues dance was inaugurated that very year at the ISTD Congress in July by the famous ballroom dancer Camille de Rhynal. Dance teachers then took the steps from the Congress and created their own variations. For example, in Liverpool the renowned dance teacher Morry Blake created the 'Blues Trot', whilst Malcolm Munro also created his own 'Blues Foxtrot'. Munro then proceeded to arrange a series of steps around a blues shape with the dance specialist Mrs Cheshire; this was presented at an Allied Dancing Association meeting at New Brighton Tower Ballroom and subsequently became a popular dance across the North of England, as dancers increasingly encountered 12- or 8-bar blues-based pieces on the dancefloor.[101]

---

[99] Stephen Cottrell, *The Saxophone* (New Haven: Yale University Press, 2013), 335.
[100] Munro, *Dancing Mad*, 102.   [101] *Ibid.*

By 28 January 1924 (the first anniversary of the Embassy Rooms) 'Marie' Daly – as Mary often styled herself professionally, the French version of the name adding a bit of showbiz glamour we assume – was being advertised in the local press as the 'leader' of the Embassy Bohemians Orchestra; a truly outstanding achievement during that decade, for a young woman in her mid-20s. The souvenir programme of that evening illustrated just how important Daly was to the entire infrastructure of an evening's entertainment. For example, not only is she named as the leader of the Embassy Bohemians in that programme but also credited, alongside Munro, as an exhibition dancer for 'The Blues' and 'The Maxixe'. During February, she was leading the Bohemians behind champion dancers Alex and Avis Moore, who had become 'The London Blues Champions' at the Professional Blues Championships held at the Princes Galleries in Piccadilly. These dancers were residents at the Embassy Rooms for four days, culminating in a 'Blues' competition on the Saturday night.[102]

By this time Liverpool had become recognised as one of *the* most important centres for ballroom dancing outside London. For example, in November 1924 Liverpool hosted the World Ballroom Dancing Championships. This competition had been organised by the influential dancer, teacher, choreographer, and competition organiser, the aforementioned French entrepreneur Camille de Rhynal, in partnership with the popular *Dancing Times* publication. The event took place at the Embassy Rooms and lasted a full week, with Daly leading the Embassy Bohemians house band throughout that week's contests and entertainments. Furthermore, as a dancer, 'Marie' Daly and her occasional dancing partner Jimmy Bird, were also awarded second place in the 'amateur' competition that took place there. According to Munro, 'it was the greatest championship event yet held in Liverpool and received striking notices in the Liverpool press.'[103] At the 1924 Blackpool Dance Festival held at the town's Winter Gardens, Daly and Munro competed in the professional dance sequence, where they presented their 'Valse Ninon' and a Paso Doble entitled 'Paso Chico'.[104]

Mary Daly's Early Radio Broadcasts

It was during the 1920s that Daly also made her first radio broadcasts. The BBC studio 6LV began transmissions from their Liverpool relay station studio on 11 June 1924. Daly recalled in the 1980s that she was one of the first artists to broadcast from this Lord Street studio, and that she would:

> [...] never forget it, when Liverpool studio opened, I said 'Oh must have a go at this, make a broadcast or something'. Anyway, we got an audition and the first song we sang was 'This is My Lucky Day.' So, we went into the

---

[102] *Ibid.*, 104.   [103] *Ibid.*, 112.   [104] *Ibid.*, 105–106.

studio, and we thought we'd do a little bit of practising on the piano, and Muriel Levy was there writing on the piano. So, we played very quietly and sung very quietly, and she said, 'Are you going to sing like that?', and I said, 'Why is it all right?' She said, 'Oh yes, it's marvellous technique that'. I had no intentions of singing like that. We were really going to belt it out. So, we kept it down and she said, 'Oh that's marvellous.'

Anyway, they gave us this fee, which was the amazing thing, for doing the audition, and when we saw the letter, we jumped up and down on Lord Street. We were delighted and we thought how bad it had been, and from then on, we did [BBC stations in] Manchester, Birmingham and Belfast.[105]

In this interview Daly did not enlarge upon who 'we' exactly were, but we assume that 'we' either refers to Daly and another member of her 'Bohemians' orchestra or perhaps more likely her occasional singing duettist Audrey Saunders.

The Charleston Arrives in Liverpool

The arrival of the Charleston on Liverpool's dancing scene was a major event. This far from discrete dance, which is thought to have originated from the 1923 US musical *Runnin' Wild*, was, during 1925, perhaps the greatest money spinner for musicians and dancing teachers alike and its banning across certain venues also greatly contributed to its popularity. Many musical revues, such as C.B. Cochrane's *On With the Dance*, featured the Charleston and innumerable new tunes were composed and copyrighted to serve its growing popularity. Such new dances also fed the status of ballroom competitions, despite them being condemned by more traditional dance instructors and associations as non-instructible. Some dance professionals were critical of the fact that many people were enthusiastically attempting the dance without proper formal instruction. However, as Munro later affirmed, the Charleston actually 'lent itself not only for judging purposes but mainly for spectacular effects on the multitude. Here indeed was a step that could be judged upon definitely, so many different styles could be done'.[106] There were often racist aspects to the criticisms concerning dancing the Charleston. It was a 'jazz' dance therefore an African American influence was at the core of its alleged lack of finesse. Writing in the *Dancing Times* in 1927, for instance, F. A. Hadland argued that a new African American dance 'had to be refined and adapted to civilized life before it could be countenanced in European ballrooms'.[107] Munro states:

---

[105] Mary Hamer, cited in Jenkins, *'Let's Go Dancing'*, 53   [106] Munro, *Dancing Mad*, 117.
[107] See James J. Nott, 'Contesting Popular Dancing and Dance Music in Britain during the 1920s', *Cultural and Social History*, Vol. 10, No. 3 (2013), 439–456.

> The writer [i.e., Munro] claims to have been the first to introduce the ballroom Charleston into the provinces following the London premiere at the Embassy Rooms on August Bank Holiday 1925, partnered by Miss Vi Thomas, a well-known amateur champion of those days. The [Embassy Bohemians] orchestra on that occasion was augmented by several members of the Chez Henri Club Orchestra who were on a visit to Liverpool.[108] [...] many of the teachers ridiculed it and many dance halls banned it. I have said over and over again that the surest way for a dance to become popular was to ban it. All the best sellers start that way. It [...] was to become one of the most popular dances of the generation [...]
>
> I will always remember one special occasion when our old friend Mr Haigh who as chairman and one of the councillors of Wavertree West Conservative Association, at their annual ball, put a request to me in these tones: "Munro, I want you and Miss Daly to show us the 'Charlestown' [sic].[109]

As discussed in Section 2, there were undoubtedly (often racist) concerns over the morality of certain genres of popular music and their accompanying dance steps, and these can easily be found in newspapers and the music and dance press of the time. However, Munro tells us that in Liverpool Charleston lessons were at a premium and, partially because of the many new dancers and teachers entering the scene during the autumn of 1925 due to this new dance's popularity, the Embassy Rooms enjoyed a record season 'not only with public dances but also with social events'.[110]

Women and the Business of Dance Band Music in the 1920s

By at least the early 1930s, several top British dance bandleaders and prominent musicians were making very good money. However, it must be stated that during the previous decade a large proportion of dance band members earned only diminutive wages (and, as we have seen, women, if employed at all earned even less). Also, it should be noted that throughout the entire interwar era paid work was not always 'regular' and that, especially during the 1920s, and, excluding noted holiday resorts such as Blackpool, the provincial rate for dance band musicians was usually far lower than those available across London and the Home Counties. It should also be stated that British propriety tended to dictate that how much a leader or a sideman was able to earn in those days was essentially considered to be a 'private matter'. Occasionally, the growing number of music-based trade papers might hint at basic rates associated with advertised work but by and large it was considered 'bad form' to openly discuss finances. The Musicians Union attempted to keep a watchful eye

---

[108] The Chez Henri Club was one of London's most famous night clubs during the 1920s.
[109] Munro, *Dancing Mad*, 116–117, 118.   [110] *Ibid.*, 118.

on members' earnings; however, it paid scant attention to female members' remunerations and requirements.

Given such scarcity of information, it is difficult to summarise how much Mary Daly was able to earn on a regular basis in her formative years as a danceband leader. One thing is certain, however: we already know that at the Embassy Rooms in Liverpool she was paid a salary of £5 per week,[111] but for how many hours during that working week as a dancer-musician, we can only speculate. It is undeniable that several male musicians in leading bands and bandleaders (such as, for example, 'Geraldo' the [aforementioned] Gerald Bright) earned extremely good salaries and commissions for their live work during the entire interwar period; those who were also able to augment their incomes with recording studio and radio work were even more fortunate. Yet, the tales of vast sums of money being earned and lost and showbusiness stories of high living perhaps belong for the most part to the 1930s. It would have to be proposed that for any less fortunate musicians – let us say those operating in the regions of the United Kingdom – rewards were only fractionally better than wages earned from more mundane occupations. Alongside professionals, semi-professional dance band musicians also existed in large numbers during the 1920s. Most semi-professionals performed on a part-time basis, some purely for fun, usually also holding down other jobs but earning additional income from playing gigs on the side. Such experienced semi-professional bands might be regularly booked by venues when full-time professionals were considered too expensive.

For example, in Liverpool, the experiences of the aforementioned semi-professional woman musician Margaret Doyle of the Liverpool-based Follies band were most likely far more typical of the wholehearted amateur dance band musicians who were 'playing with a small group of like-minded friends, reading from commercially arranged scores, rehearsing every week in a front parlour, and playing at myriad small hops and dances around the city'.[112] Therefore, although the 1930s are (rightly, in many respects – particularly in a financial sense) regarded as the 'golden years' of the dance band era, the 1920s were financially 'formative', at best – especially for those few women involved in dance bands. Mary Daly, as an acknowledged professional bandleader, was indeed a rare exception.

4 Move to the Grafton Rooms: Old Tyme Nights and the Built Environment

As we have seen, by the mid-1920s the Embassy Rooms were doing extremely well. In 1924, however, a significant competitor arrived on the scene when the Grafton Rooms, situated on West Derby Road, Liverpool, opened its doors on

---

[111] £5 in 1925 would be worth just over £380 in 2024.   [112] Jenkins, *'Let's Go Dancing'*, 44.

Saturday 9 February. An article in the *Liverpool Echo* warmly welcomed the new venue:

> It has often been remarked that while Liverpool possesses many well-equipped dance halls, it has lacked a really big establishment for dancing. That reproach, however, is now removed, for on Saturday afternoon the new Grafton rooms in West Derby Road, were opened to the public for the first time. The new rooms (next door to the Olympia) may truly be described as a Palais de Danse, for only on Saturday afternoon fully 1,600 people attended, and yet the floor never presented the 'crush' that so often mars a popular dance. What I like about the new dance hall was its spacious openness. Everything has been arranged with a view of accommodating crowds, and those with responsibility for the planning have done their work excellently [...] This is a tribute to the architect (Mr A.E. Shennon), and to the managing directors, both of them with profound experience of the real requirements needed in a building where crowds are expected. Both Mr Pierre Cohen and Mr F.E. Weisker, and the other members of the board are to be congratulated.[113]

That first night of the Grafton Rooms was a phenomenal success. Doors opened at 6.30pm and within the hour the capacity of 1,600 had been reached. This perhaps unexpected 'full house' even prompted the Grafton management to place an apology in the *Liverpool Echo* the following Tuesday: 'The Directorate tender their regrets that many were unable to gain admission on Saturday night. The capacity was reached by 7.15[pm]. 1,500 people having paid admission.'[114] With full houses quickly becoming a regular feature of the Grafton Rooms, the venue swiftly garnered a reputation as *the* leading ballroom dancing venue in Liverpool and appeared to be going from strength to strength. However, a great deal of money had been invested in this new venture. Building costs had been vast and with the infrastructure extravagant and the venue perhaps over-staffed, profits could be thin and at times non-existent. This section discusses the re-location of Munro, Daly, and Hamer to the Grafton Rooms in 1927/28 and analyses how they built upon their already established reputations as leaders within Liverpool's popular music and dance scene to cement the Grafton Rooms as the premier venue for ballroom dancing in Liverpool and Merseyside.

Malcolm Munro's Growing Reputation

Despite the Grafton's rising influence across Liverpool's dancing fraternity, so strong was the Embassy Rooms' reputation that in September 1926 Munro had booked the famous ballroom dancing partners Josephine Bradley ('The First

---

[113] Anonymous, 'Liverpool's Biggest Dance Hall Opens'.
[114] Anonymous, 'Pas de Trios', *Liverpool Echo* (12 February 1924), n.p.

Lady of the Ballroom', 1893–1985) and Douglas Wellesley-Smith to visit Merseyside. Bradley and Wellesley-Smith had only been dancing partners since 1924; however, Bradley had already won the World Foxtrot Championship with her previous partner the American, G.K. Anderson. The pair not only gave a lecture demonstration at the Dancers' Circle in Liverpool on the Saturday afternoon of their visit but followed this with demonstrations at the Embassy Rooms on the Saturday and the Assembly Rooms in New Brighton on the following Monday evening. Munro's influence across the ballroom dancing world was growing apace of the popularity of ballroom dancing and by bringing this famous pair to Liverpool – Bradley had already opened a dance studio in London and was regarded as one of the foremost dance teachers of the era[115] – the young manager did his organisational reputation no harm whatsoever.

In fact, so influential had Malcolm Munro become that he was invited to Paris the following year (May 1927) to adjudicate at the World Dancing Championships. Following his return, he then also helped open a new ballroom adjoining the Bath Hotel in Leamington Spa. It is not known whether Munro was financially involved in this venture, but he certainly assembled the resident band for the new venue, which was led by his younger brother Wilf Hamer: at that time still in his teens. Hamer also included in this new band his older brother, Vincent, and Mary Daly. She was employed as relief dance pianist and as dance hostess and exhibition partner to Munro. Munro comments: 'Her interludes were justly popular.'[116] This ballroom in Leamington Spa soon became one of the most important venues for locals and visitors-alike and Munro recalls that he did not 'remember a ballroom with a more sparkling and cosmopolitan atmosphere than the Bath [Hotel] Assembly Rooms. Later designated the Palais, with its great number of wealthy Americans and continental visitors, to see them dancing up to 4 o'clock in the morning, it was just like Paris or the Riviera'.[117]

Meanwhile, back in Liverpool in 1927 new ballrooms were rapidly opening to cater for the ever-growing ballroom dancing craze, placing pressure on the Grafton Rooms. For example, just as the Rialto opened on the corner of Berkeley Street and Upper Parliament Street on 7 October that year at a cost of £57,000, another palatial venue, named the Casino, was also erected in Kensington – this latter ballroom was in fact only a short distance from the Grafton Rooms. Such new establishments (together with several existing dance halls and cafés, such as The State and the Woolton Assembly Rooms) gradually emerged as a challenge to the dominance of the Grafton Rooms. The Embassy Rooms, meanwhile, persevered despite the

---

[115] By 1924 Bradley had already started her first dance school: in the Knightsbridge Hotel. She was one of the most famous British ballroom dancers of the twentieth century, and heavily involved in the ISTD's efforts to codify ballroom dance steps (discussed in Section 2).

[116] Munro, *Dancing Mad*, 123.   [117] *Ibid.*, 124.

occasional absence of Munro, Daly, and Hamer – all gainfully employed elsewhere (for example in Leamington Spa).

New Management at the Grafton

Despite such healthy competition, the Grafton's supremacy seldom appeared in doubt – at least in the minds of the general public. However, behind the scenes poor management and accounting had meant that the Grafton's limited company was making heavy losses. The directors of the Grafton therefore decided that a venue manager with his finger on the ballroom dancing pulse was required to turn around such losses. Malcolm Munro's organisational reputation was by this time preceding him and prior to the autumn 1927 season he was approached by Grafton Rooms managing director Fred Weisker. During 1926 and 1927 Munro had in fact been spending a great deal of time away from Liverpool, having visited Paris on at least two occasions, London we think several times, and had, as illustrated earlier, assisted developing the new Bath Hotel Assembly Rooms in Leamington Spa. All of this suggests that he might have already been on the lookout for new opportunities away from the Embassy Rooms. Following Weisker's approach, Munro was interviewed and formally offered the manager's job by the largest shareholder in the company, Mrs Higgins. Both Weisker and Higgins viewed Munro as the man capable of turning the Grafton's losses into profit. By November 1927 Munro had accepted the offer of managing the Grafton Rooms. From extant Grafton Rooms programmes, it appears that he had also taken on the additional responsibility of being licensee by at least the mid-1930s.[118]

Nevertheless, during his first few weeks in his new role as manager, he came to realise that the venue was in serious financial difficulties. He in fact discovered a huge debt of over £12,000 together with a further £5,000 mortgage; there also existed a bank overdraft of more than £8,000 in dire need of servicing.[119] Therefore, unlike the *Liverpool Echo* reporter quoted earlier, Munro soon discovered the reality of, rather than the fantasy surrounding, the Grafton Rooms. For example, as it turned out, it was a rather poorly constructed and partly unfinished building. The Grafton Rooms undoubtedly looked good and for its many punters probably felt like a fantastic environment in which one might escape the day-to-day mundanity of Liverpool. The layers of opulence were illusionary and beneath lay serious infrastructure problems which demanded an immediate and systematic diversion of the Grafton's revenue streams. The directors were duly informed: their hoped-for dividends would have to wait.

---

[118] 'Liverpool's Popular Palais', Grafton Rooms Programme (1934); Liverpool Central Library and Archives, Shelf Mark: H793.33 GRA.

[119] Munro, *Dancing Mad*, 124–125.

In his autobiography Munro informs us that he decided to face 'head-on' these structural and financial issues and immediately set about attempting to bring both finances and infrastructure in line with the Grafton Rooms' reputation as a state-of-the-art ballroom. Although Munro wrote that he initially felt that he had made one of the biggest mistakes of his life in joining what appeared to him to be a failing company, by October of the following year (1928) he had achieved for the company at least some degree of solvency and building safety without the dancing public ever knowing about the precarious structural and financial state of the venue. He stated:

> Being entirely ignorant of the tortuous ways of high finance [...] I was working my brains away to pay off interest and directors fees, with scarcely anything left over for shareholders and the maintenance costs. With the advent of new ballrooms, competition was very fierce, which delighted me in those days – it kept me alert – but I don't think I would like to go through the same formula again. At one period we were paying £100 per month off the bank overdraft, which was far too much in those days of falling prices. It absolutely soaked the place; the fabric of the building could have done with half that amount at least, instead of being allowed to deteriorate as it was. In modern concepts the Grafton was a bad and unfinished building with the exception of a large dancing space and fortunately a very good sprung floor.[120]

For the first twelve months of Munro's management Monty Wilson's Commanders had been contracted as the Grafton's house band. They had been resident at the venue prior to Munro's arrival. 'Monty Wilson' was in fact Tommy Wilson and had brought his band to Liverpool from Edinburgh. Although Monty Wilson's Commanders were costing the Grafton a considerable amount of money, they were considered a good, reliable band. So much so, in fact, that after impressing local ballroom dancer, dance promoter, and master of ceremonies Jack (S. J.) Fallon,[121] at Liverpool's first Ancient Order of Foxtrotters (AOFT) Festival at the Grafton in May 1928,[122] Wilson and his band were offered by Fallon a lucrative contract to become residents at his (Fallon's) new ballroom in Bolton: the Bolton Palais.[123] Given the Grafton's possible 'penny pinching' at that time, Tommy Wilson's departure, although embarrassing for both Munro and the Grafton management, might have come as something of a financial relief. When Fallon's offer was duly accepted by Wilson, Munro turned to his younger brother Wilf Hamer, who by this time had left the Embassy Rooms in Mount Pleasant and

---

[120] *Ibid.*, 124–125.
[121] N.b. **Not** the Canadian Jack Fallon who became a well-known jazz and rock 'n' roll entrepreneur.
[122] The Ancient Order of Foxtrotters was formed in 1928 to improve and popularise the 'slow-time' foxtrot; over 6,000 members were enrolled in its first year.
[123] Fallon also later became manager of the Nottingham Palais and a renowned London impresario.

was playing first alto sax in Billy Page's Band at the Palais in Douglas, Isle of Man. Wilf agreed to help his brother and hurriedly formed a small band consisting of only eight players under the title 'Wilf Hamer's Atlanta Dance Orchestra'. We do not know whether Daly had joined Wilf in the Isle of Man, but we think they were perhaps already romantically involved by this point. Munro was to later write of Wilf Hamer's new band:

> This famous combination of dance musicians continued with few changes of personnel from October 1928 to January 1956, with the exception of one season at Tony's Ballroom, Birmingham, one season at the Palais De Danse, Nottingham, five summers at the Queen's Dance Hall, Rhyl, North Wales, and one summer season at Payne's Majestic, Llandudno.[124] When Wilf Hamer died in 1936, his wife Mary, known to many thousands of dancers as Marie Daly who as previously mentioned [...] was leader of the 'Embassy Bohemians' at the Embassy Rooms and a noted dance pianist, took over the leadership of the orchestra and continued, with a minor break [...] in 1948, until it disbanded in January 1956.[125]

The Grafton Rooms and Wilf Hamer's 'Old-Time (Olde-Tyme) Nights'

Looking back in his memoirs, Malcolm Munro was to later state that the 1928–1929 dance season was for him one of 'melancholy' as he attempted to establish a specialised niche for the Grafton within Liverpool's fiercely competitive dance music marketplace. As it turned out, Wilf Hamer's 'quick solution' band, which included Mary Daly as pianist, turned out to be an excellent choice to replace Monty Wilson's Commanders, for they were versatile and informed concerning ballroom trends. Playing at the second AOFT festival in December 1928 and with a reputation beginning to precede them to 'those in the know', the Hamer band created an all-round good impression amongst dancers and judges alike. The band apparently displayed great versatility when playing behind champion dancers Josephine Bradley and Douglas Wellesley-Smith who performed a contemporary dance to the strains of George Olsen's 'Varsity Drag' – an interesting piece of jazzy US ragtime pop which 'gave us a foretaste of what the teenagers would demand in the near future'.[126]

But the Wilf Hamer Band were even more versatile than this. Back in February 1928 – on Tuesday, 14th, St Valentine's Night – Munro had presented a feature evening entitled *'Ye Olde Tyme' Valentine Revel*, which had comprised several old-time dances, such as waltzes and veletas, set to modern arrangements

---

[124] It is noteworthy that all of the venues mentioned were amongst the most well-known of the period. It offers further testimony of the calibre of the Grafton Rooms house band.
[125] Munro, *Dancing Mad*, 128.   [126] Munro, *Dancing Mad*, 129.

by Wilf Hamer and Mary Daly. The highlight of the evening was a burlesque polka exhibited by 'Marie' Daly, Topsy Steele (another former Embassy Rooms colleague), and Munro himself. As Munro later recollected:

> I used to say to myself, in show business as in every other business we must not go back, we must go forward, we must progress. However, I realised that there was a definite public for old-time dances, and the number of requests which reached me after my first venture increased that belief. Also, I had noticed how popular certain old tunes were, when occasionally revived by the dance bands, such as 'Daisy', 'Lily of Laguna', 'You Made Me Love You', 'Alexander's Ragtime Band' and many more. I promised to consider the matter carefully, because it was a big risk for a modern ballroom to make. We wanted to keep both the moderns and the old-timers interested and it was not until the following year, on St Valentine's Night, Thursday February 14th, 1929, that I definitely decided to launch a genuine old-time night.'[127]

Together Hamer and Daly set about rearranging an extensive assortment of Victorian and Edwardian dances – including veletas, lancers, barn dances, military two-steps, polkas, and waltzes – for interwar dance band syncopation. There was, according to Munro, a growing national interest in such older repertories; therefore, both he and the band decided that 'Liverpool [should] take a leading part in this back to the beginning movement [although] the famous popular "Old Time Repertory" nights [really] evolved through a fortuitous accident'.[128] We will never know just how much Munro places himself at the centre of this narrative, as 'old-tyme' quickly became a marked ballroom trend across the UK with several different dance halls claiming to have been the first to introduce it. Although an anonymous writer in a December 1935 edition of *Dance Band Diaries* backed Munro's claims by asserting that the 'big revival in old-time dance-music is largely attributed to Malcolm Munro, manager of Liverpool's Grafton Rooms',[129] for instance, the next week's edition of the same trade paper noted 'old-time dance controversy spreads' and asked 'who started the revival' noting that there were several 'provincial' claims.[130] Whatever the case, the Grafton Rooms certainly became an important focal point for the old-time trend in the North and Nott has also asserted that 'Malcolm Munro at the Grafton, Liverpool [...] led the revival'.[131] The decision to create an 'old-time' evening programme does seem, however, to have been a joint effort between Munro, Hamer, and Daly, rather than Munro alone. In fact, Munro does confess to the reader that Wilf Hamer 'had always been at me to run an old-time night',[132] and Wilf may have been working on

---

[127] *Ibid.*, 130.   [128] *Ibid.*, 129.
[129] Anonymous, Untitled, *Dance Band Diaries* (14 December 1935), 3.
[130] Anonymous, Untitled, *Dance Band Diaries* (21 December 1935), 5.
[131] Nott, *Going to the Palais*, 117.   [132] Munro, *Dancing Mad*, 131.

such arrangements for quite some time. During his time playing for Tom Hayton in Manchester, Wilf Hamer had noted that Hayton had also liked to run the occasional old-time night. Apparently, Hayton had reams of old orchestrations which were of little-to-no use to his band of contemporary musicians, many of whom found them somewhat difficult to read, never mind rearrange. Instead, the band simply busked their way through them in a relaxed contemporary style. The tunes were most likely well known to all and sundry in any case. It was this, stated Munro, that 'gave Wilf a brainwave, why not re-orchestrate the old tunes to suit modern instrumentation [...] and the famous "Hamer's Melodious Memories" was born'.[133] Alongside Mary Daly's ever-present piano and professional knowledge of the dancefloor, Hamer's band used three saxophones, three brass, and three rhythm instruments. Modern harmonies – such as blues influenced flattened sevenths together with the ubiquitous minor sixth – were also used to effectively bring these old yet well-loved tunes up to date. It must have sounded great fun, perhaps even at times a little riotous! Figure 3 reproduces a caricature of Wilf Hamer's Band ('Hamer and His Music') in 1933, including Mary Hamer on the piano.

Figure 3 Hamer and His Music (1933). Courtesy of Liverpool Central Library and Archives.

---

[133] *Ibid.*, 131.

Bandleader Mrs Mary Hamer and Her Boys 45

In one of the very rare references to the pre–Second World War Grafton Rooms in wider popular music historical literature, Nott has commented that 'the manager of the Grafton Rooms, Liverpool [Munro], had charabanc parties from all over Lancashire visiting his twice weekly old-time dances'.[134] Certainly, by 1932 the *Liverpool Echo* dance columnist was suggesting that dancers were travelling great distances to experience the Grafton's 'Olde-Tyme' nights:

> Liverpool is becoming a centre for old-time dance enthusiasts, and I learnt from Mr Malcolm Munro, of the Grafton Rooms, that patrons come from as far afield as Fleetwood and Hanley to the Tuesday and Thursday gatherings at this hall. Perhaps we shall soon have 'Olde Tyme' excursion trains.
>
> Much of the success of these dances is due to the delightful orchestrations by Hamer and his band.[135]

The trio of Munro, Hamer, and Daly all functioned as extremely important trendsetters in the late 1920s. They effectively established a hybrid genre which later grew into a significant popular music trend: that of the 1930s old-time dancing revival. This 'revival' in fact extended well into the 1960s with old-time presentations featuring in competition dancing, television programmes (such as those featured in *Come Dancing* and *The Good Old Days*), and across BBC national and local radio networks. When BBC Radio Merseyside commenced broadcasting in 1967, *Music and Memories from the 1930s* became part of their weekly schedule. George Hamer has also informed us that the 'Olde-Tyme' Nights at the Grafton Rooms continued well into the 1950s.[136] Nott has asserted that:

> 'Old-Time Dancing' gained vogue in the mid-1930s and many dance halls provided a programme of old-style music at least once a week. Some dance halls even began to cater exclusively for this sort of dancing. At these evenings, older patrons, from middle age to old age, would rub shoulders with the young. It provided a 'family atmosphere' and was very popular.[137]

Despite its general association with the mid-1930s, this new vogue for old-time dancing was firmly set in motion at the Grafton Rooms on Tuesday, 14 February 1929. Each subsequent Tuesday (and later, also Thursdays) up to 1,000 people attended. This old-time revival trend – although initiated in Liverpool at the Grafton Rooms – caught hold across the UK. For example, Nott names the Oxford Galleries in Newcastle; the Leeds Palais-de Danse; the Marine Gardens, Edinburgh; Jack Fallon's Nottingham Palais-de-Danse; and Tony's Ballroom in Birmingham as all hosting successful old-time nights.[138]

---

[134] Nott, *Music for the People*, 182.
[135] Anonymous, 'Old-Time Enthusiasm', *Liverpool Echo* (1932), n.p.
[136] Source: George Hamer.   [137] Nott, *Music for the People*, 182.   [138] *Ibid*.

Geraldo also followed suit and created his well-loved BBC Light Programme radio series of old-time dancing numbers, entitled *Dancing Through*.

In addition to establishing an important specialism at the Grafton Rooms, Hamer, Daly, and Munro's concept might have also been inspired by the fact that a significant number of dancers were anxious about the greater degrees of freedom which characterised the new 'jazz' dances of the 1920s and perhaps missed the more formalised nature of the dances of the Victorian and Edwardian period. As Tackley has commented, 'The increasingly improvisational nature of modern jazz dancing made this style intimidating for dancers used to the previously strict conventions of ballroom dancing.'[139]

However, it should also be noted that, at least at the Grafton Rooms, these old-time pieces were in fact somewhat syncopated, thus allowing a perhaps more modern 'texture' to sit behind the nineteenth-century musical settings. Either way, the establishment of 'Old Time Nights' responded to a very distinct need for an interwar old-time dance scene, something recognised and then instigated by Munro, Hamer, and Daly. In a financial sense the 'Old Time Nights' also helped to further consolidate the Grafton Rooms as, not only the most patronised ballroom in Liverpool, but also the venue housing the most successful band of this genre in that era. Munro writes: 'Wilf Hamer and his Band, then at the Grafton Rooms, were winning golden opinions for their modern dance playing, particularly of the slow foxtrot and Miss Josephine Bradley, in a letter which I still treasure, declared them to be the best foxtrot band in the country.'[140] The Old-Time nights frequently carried themes, as Munro recollected:

> 'The Bridge of Athlone' on St Patrick's Night, 'The Grand March Lancers' on Armistice Night, November 11th, for many years a notable event. There were never to be forgotten Hallowe'en nights with its 'ghosts, gnomes, witches, goblins and hob-goblins' […] Then we had 'Flora Dora Nights' with the lovely melodies of Leslie Stuart […] 'Gaiety Nights', 'Daly's Nights', 'Spanish Fiestas', 'Nautical Nights' were often featured.[141]

Naturally, such popularity, together with other promotions such as 'novelty nights' (an early incarnation of talent competitions), ballroom competitions, and official championship dancing nights not only helped Munro balance the Grafton's books, but also made the venue nationally renowned. Munro was later to declare:

> […] it was the means whereby £4,000 was paid off the Grafton overdraft in a few years, from about thirteen thousand pounds to just over eight thousand

---

[139] Parsonage, *The Evolution of Jazz in Britain*, 19.   [140] Munro, *Dancing Mad*, 130–131.

[141] Munro, *Dancing Mad*, 135. Audrey McKinnell recollects 'Daly's Nights' continuing later in the 1930s, when Daly would not only select the material and lead the band but also dance her way around the floor.

pounds. The old-time revival spread like wildfire, not only through Liverpool and district, but all over the country. Teachers came from far and near, dance promoters, dance hall directors and proprietors of companies came to see this new-fangled creation [but] it scarcely touched London, and that great city had to wait about ten years for an old-time revival until Harry Davidson and his broadcasting feature 'Those Were the Days' was radioed all over the British Isles. How slow the BBC were to broadcast this famous revival.[142]

BBC Broadcasts and Family Matters

The Wilf Hamer Band finally made their first radio broadcast for the BBC North Region in November 1935.[143] The band received another transmission on 12 December ('Melodious Memories'). Following which, *Radio Pictorial* was to remark a little later in February 1936: 'General conclusions that can be drawn from the results are that old-fashioned dance-music at least holds its own with modern jazz. Geraldo's "Dancing Through" and Hamer's "Old-Time Dance Tunes" had three times as many votes as Ambrose, Henry Hall and Jack Payne.'[144] There were further broadcasts in 1936, one of which was on St Patrick's Night (17th March), and others on 30th November and New Year's Eve. By the time of these latter two broadcasts the band was led by Mary Hamer (as discussed in Section 5). All such broadcasts were of course *several* years after the old-time genre's initial impact at the Grafton in Liverpool.

Mary Daly and Wilf Hamer married in 1931. First son Ian was born in 1932, second son Stewart in 1934 – which may have led to Mary temporarily leaving the band and the Hamer Band altering their residencies at the Grafton, somewhat – and third son George was born in 1936.

Wilf Hamer Band's Residency at Tony's Ballroom, Birmingham

In November 1933 it was reported locally that Wilf Hamer's Band was to leave the Grafton for a five-month stint at Tony's Ballroom in Birmingham followed by another five months at the Nottingham Palais de Danse. (Like the Grafton Rooms, both Tony's Ballroom, Birmingham, and the Nottingham Palais de Danse were renowned provincial venues.) Munro much later penned in glowing terms the Wilf Hamer Band's last night (at least for some time) at the Grafton Rooms:

---

[142] *Ibid*. 132.
[143] *Ibid*. The BBC Genome Project gives the date as 15 May 1936. See Broadcast– BBC Programme Index (last accessed 29 October 2024).
[144] Anonymous, *Radio Pictorial* (week of 7 February 1936), n.p. Presumably listeners were invited to vote for their favourite dance bands.

> A memorable event on Friday, November 10th [1933] when we said *au revoir* to Wilf Hamer and his Band. They had established a record for an all-the-year-round dance by staying with us for five years and they had earned eulogistic tributes from the press both local and professional, from famous London exhibition dancers and from patrons and visitors from all over the world. Under the guidance of the genial Wilf they, in no small measure, had been responsible for the wonderful popularity of the 'Olde Tyme' nights, the revival of which gave a lead to the country, while their brilliantly played tango numbers not only started a vogue for the dance here, but brought them glowing tributes from all critics, including Mr Victor Silvester, who said they were one of the best tango bands in the country […][145]

The Wilf Hamer Band thrilled audiences and reviewers-alike across the West Midlands, especially via Hamer's proficiency on the Argentinian bandoneon. The press picked up on his expertise. For example, the *Birmingham Daily Post* correspondent was moved to write:

> **THE BANDONEON COMES TO BIRMINGHAM**
> **NOVEL BAND INSTRUMENT**
> One distinction possessed by Mr. Wilf Hamer, whose band, recently installed at Tony's Ballroom, Birmingham, has quickly made a hit with local dancers, is that he is one of the few men in this country who is expert with the bandoneon, an Argentine accordion instrument, which can be of great value in modern dance music.
>
> Mr Christopher Stone, of BBC gramophone broadcasting fame, was struck with the accomplishment when he heard the band in Liverpool some time ago and got Mr Hamer to give him a demonstration. Not long previously the leader of a famous London tango band had assured Mr Stone that it was impossible to get a bandoneon player in England, and that he could not get a permit to bring an Argentine player into this country. Consequently, Mr Stone was astonished to find an Englishman handling the instrument in Liverpool.
>
> Mr Hamer and his band were so popular on Merseyside that they put in five years at that mecca of local dancing – the Grafton Rooms. Their selection for Birmingham was a sequel to a careful search, in the course of which the management of Tony's heard scores of bands before determining their choice of successor to Mr Syd Dean's combination. One of the most important dances at which the band will figure during next month will be Birmingham's press Ball, which is to be held at Tony's on December 19.[146]

---

[145] Munro, *Dancing Mad*, 147. During their residency at Tony' Ballroom, Birmingham, Wilf Hamer's Band were replaced at the Grafton Rooms by a band formed by Jack Fallon, Roy's Commanders (which was under the musical direction of the percussionist, Roy Richards).

[146] Anonymous, 'Day to Day', *Birmingham Daily Post* (November 1933), n.p.

Return to the Grafton Rooms

Wilf Hamer and his band returned to the Grafton on August Bank Holiday 1934; however, the venue was somewhat different, for by this time it was truly nationally known. In 1932 Louis Armstrong played the Grafton on his first visit to the UK – an interesting historical indicator of the growing popularity of 'hot' jazz. The following year, 1933, Duke Ellington arrived in Liverpool for a week's engagement at the Liverpool Empire. On the Friday night Ellington and his band went on to the Grafton and played (or, according to some sources 'jammed') there. For some decades thereafter Ellington and his band's appearance at the Grafton became part of Liverpool's popular music folklore. The band arrived at the Grafton from the Empire (only a short taxi ride away) circa midnight and played until three o'clock the following morning. Mary Hamer later recalled:

> I wasn't playing when Duke Ellington came but I was there. I thought it was the most marvellous band, because they *ad libbed* the whole time they were there. They were calling across to Duke, he was in his heyday then, and he played '[Mood] Indigo', 'Sophisticated Lady', all those lovely tunes, gorgeous things.[147]

Although African American musicians were popular in the city, few Black Liverpudlians were welcomed at most of the city's venues, which remained deeply racist. Black Liverpudlian Grace Wilkie recalled that she 'used to go to the Grafton. Black people weren't too popular, but during the war they relaxed. [However,] The Rialto was something else, because Blacks didn't get in there'.[148] Former leader of the Chants vocal group Joe Ankrah informed Mike Brocken that he went to the Grafton as a young man (probably in the late 1950s or early1960s) but was assaulted outside the venue.[149] Ironically, Joe later sang there: at first with the Chants and then later with his wife as a member of the Grafton house band.

Throughout the 1930s, the Grafton Rooms also regularly hosted several British 'big name bands' as leading attractions. For example, the various bands of Lew Stone with Al Bowlly as vocalist, those led by Roy Fox, Billy Cotton, Debroy Somers, and both Jack Hylton and Mrs Jack Hylton Bands, amongst many others, appeared at the venue whilst the Wilf Hamer Band was away. This was often during the summer months; from 1935 the Hamer Band were regularly engaged for the summer season at the Queen's Dance Hall at the (then) popular summer tourist destination of Rhyl, North Wales.[150] These famous bands were playing the Grafton quite simply because the venue held national prominence as a dance music mecca.

---

[147] Mary Hamer cited from Jenkins, *'Let's Go Dancing'*, 36.   [148] *Ibid.*, 37.
[149] Joe Ankrah in interview with Mike Brocken, June 2010.
[150] For an important study of popular music in mid-nineteenth- to mid-twentieth-century Wales, see Jen Wilson, *Freedom Music: Wales, Emancipation and Jazz, 1850–1950* (Cardiff: University of Wales Press, 2019).

Wilf Hamer's Approach to Dance Band Leadership

In the mid-1930s, Wilf Hamer wrote an illuminating article for the *Liverpool Echo* on his approach to dance band leading which it is worth quoting at length:

Dancing on Merseyside.
The Band's Point of View; Getting the Atmosphere;
The Ideal Combination
By Wilf Hamer, Leader of Grafton Rooms Band

The public little realise as they dance to the strains of a good band, the forethought, preparation, and scrupulous attention to the smallest detail the leader or musical director must put in before the flowing melody at the correct tempo is produced.

The first essential is to gauge the atmosphere in which his band is to play. Discrimination must be made between playing in a Palais-de-danse and at a restaurant. Dancing is the first and only consideration in the Palais; in the restaurant it is secondary to food and wine.

Having played for four years in a hall where the standard of dancing has been highly praised by leading experts, I feel I can suggest what the public requires from the dance band. Good melody with a strongly marked rhythm is most acceptable to the average dancer, with occasional "hot" arrangements of well-known tunes. Generally, we play all dances at Official Board tempos,[151] but occasionally we vary these to obtain greater elasticity.

'Hot' Numbers and Tangoes.

'Hot' playing is an art in itself, and, if not supervised carefully, is open to abuse by musicians whose enthusiasm outruns their ability. I take great care in arranging numbers of this description, and every member of my band plays from a written copy where we feature a special number.[152]

I am convinced that the praise which my band has received from experts with regard to our tango tempo is due, in no small measure to the strict attention to detail which I endeavour to give each number. Few realise, when they see the bandsmen lay down their brass and reed instruments and take up bandoneons, accordions, violins, and a string bass, that a special part has to be written for each instrument, and that a number which takes, perhaps, three or four minutes to play, had been carefully rehearsed for two or three days.

The need for careful orchestration is also called for in the arrangement of numbers for 'Old Tyme' dances. The majority of the published orchestral parts from bygone days are unsuitable for the instrumentation of the modern band, and as it is only through suitable music rendered in attractive style that dancing lives, a dance band leader must devise his own arrangements.

---

[151] Presumably, here Wilf Hamer is referring to the 'strict tempos' approved by the ISTD, which became one of the bedrocks of the 'English' ballroom style.

[152] It is possible that the Hamer-Munro family hold some extant scores within the family archives.

The Ideal Combination.

The combination of a band can make or mar a leader's reputation. Naturally, it has to suit the capacity of the ballroom in which it will play. My ideal combination, based on a dancing capacity of 1,000 people, is: two pianos, two alto and two tenor saxophones (doubling on clarinets, baritons [sic] and violins); two trumpets (one doubling violin and one doubling piano); two trombones, drums, bass, violin, and banjo (doubling guitar). At least four members of the band would be vocalists and would feature four-part harmony singing.[153]

Of particular significance here are Wilf Hamer's comments on how to create 'what the public requires from the dance band': correct tempos and strong melodies and rhythms. It is interesting to note that he effectively prevented his band from improvising during 'hot' numbers (as they might otherwise have been tempted so to do) by providing them with written-out parts and insisting that they stuck to them. His observations also highlight another two key issues within contemporary dance music: the 'hot' versus 'sweet' debate – especially prevalent in the 1930s[154] – and how dance music was aesthetically understood at the time. From the 1920s, popular music had been polarised into 'sweet' British dance music and 'hot' Black American jazz music. Wilf Hamer's insistence that his band curb their enthusiasm for 'hot' sounds when playing for dances at the Grafton certainly highlights his keen understanding of what the public expected when they visited the Grafton Rooms: sweet music – usually of the ballroom genre – to which they could dance.

5 Taking over the Band: Mrs Wilf Hamer and Her Boys, Strategies of Female Dance Band Leadership

Unfortunately, tragedy struck the Hamer family in July 1936, when Wilf died after catching pneumonia working a summer season with the Grafton Rooms dance band at the Queen's Dance Hall in Rhyl (North Wales). Mary Hamer had just given birth to their third son, George, and was recovering in a nursing home when he died. However, as Munro recollected in his autobiography:

> Marie Daly [. . .] took over her husband's baton in Rhyl in best 'show goes on' tradition, and returned to the Grafton in October as Mrs. Wilf Hamer. Broadcasting in the North region on November 30th and again on December 31st, New Year's Eve they made an outstanding success of a cavalcade of Merseyside Pantomime tunes.[155]

---

[153] Wilf Hamer, 'Dancing on Merseyside: The Band's Point of View; Getting the Atmosphere; The Ideal Combination', *Liverpool Echo* (c.mid-1930s; Hamer-Munro Archives), n.p.

[154] The 'hot' versus 'sweet' debate was keenly covered in the British popular music trade press. Recordings and sheet music of this time were habitually marketed as 'hot' or 'sweet'.

[155] Munro, *Dancing Mad*, 154.

Affirming Wilf Hamer's fame, his premature death was reported as a 'Stop Press' item on 18 July 1936 in *Melody Maker*, which advised readers that 'Wilf Hamer, noted Liverpool band-leader, died from pneumonia. His band at Queen's Dance Hall, Rhyl, is now being conducted by his widow, Marie Daly'.[156] Thus, at a time when working women were a rarity, Mary Hamer took up her husband's former position as leader. She continued – with only a minor break of around two years in the late 1940s, when she ran her own ballroom: The Star Ballroom in Wallasey – until the band disbanded in the mid-1950s. This section discusses Mary Hamer's leadership of the band during this period, and the various strategies which she adopted to assert her position as a woman leader on the bandstand.

Mrs Wilf Hamer and Her Band

Intriguingly, after Mary Hamer took over, the band became known as 'Mrs Wilf Hamer's Band'. It was also sometimes (seemingly interchangeably) referred to as 'Mrs Wilf Hamer and Her Boys', rather than Mary Hamer's Band. The preservation of Wilf's name within the band's – as well as likely serving as a kind of tribute and memorial to him – may also have helped to downplay any perceived female threat. It should also be remembered, however, that bands of this period more often than not took their take from their leader; famous examples include Jack Hylton and his Orchestra and the Lou Stone Orchestra. Given that, as discussed in Section 2, professional female dancers and, to an extent, also musicians were still viewed as morally suspicious during the interwar period, the title Mrs was a cast-iron guarantee of respectability. It is also important to note that the Grafton Room's house band was already famous and very well established as Wilf Hamer's Band when Mary Hamer took over the leadership, so the practical consideration of retaining this well-known 'brand' played a part in the decision – presumably taken by Munro, who was an extremely acute businessman – not to change the name.

However, it is also possible that the name 'Mrs Wilf Hamer and her Band' might have been at least partly inspired by the short-lived success of Mrs Jack Hylton and her Band (active 1933–1937). This band was led by Ennis Parkes (Florence Ennis Parkinson, 1893–1957), the former wife of one of Britain's most successful and well-known bandleaders, Jack Hylton (1892–1965). In the case of Parkes' band, the use of her famous former spouse's name was an obvious marketing strategy, which certainly worked for a while as her band achieved considerable success, including high-profile engagements, recording contracts, and extensive press coverage.[157] As Munro's autobiography makes

---

[156] Anonymous, 'Stop Press', *Melody Maker*, Vol. 7, No. 9 (18 July 1936), 2.

[157] Ennis Parkes' decision to continue to style herself as 'Mrs Jack Hylton' was somewhat ironic, given that the couple had actually divorced in 1929 (although they remained good friends).

clear, he knew Hylton – a close contemporary in age – well. As noted in Section 4, both Hylton and Mrs Jack Hylton appeared with their bands as guest artists at the Grafton Rooms many times throughout the 1930s. It is quite possible that Munro was influenced by the success of Mrs Jack Hylton's Band, which he would have been aware of. In interview with Mike Brocken in the late 1990s Clive Garner was also of the opinion that the moniker of 'Mrs Wilf Hamer's Band' was 'undoubtedly influenced by the success of Mrs Jack Hylton's Band. The precedent had been set and because Mrs Hylton's Band was very successful and the members could be interchangeable with Jack's Band, it seemed a good move.'[158]

Speaking on BBC Radio Merseyside in the 1980s, Mary Hamer revealed that she did have certain reservations about taking on her husband's former job:

> Mr Weisker gave me the job. He asked me would I take the band over. So I said 'Yes, thank you very much', and then I started to think of the implications of taking a band over with all men and how they would take to it, and some of them didn't take too kindly to it. They thought it wouldn't succeed and a lot of people wrote asking could they take the band over and we didn't give them a chance, I don't think. They said I couldn't make a success of it as it wasn't generally accepted, let's face it, to have a lady in front of an all-male band.[159] But to me it was nothing new because I'd been in it from my school days really, you might say, from thirteen.[160]

This suggestion of some internal resistance from within the band to Mary Hamer's appointment to succeed her husband is intriguing. Gender issues aside, it was not uncommon within dance band culture for a current senior professional to take over a leadership position, when a bandleader moved on. Therefore Munro, Weisker, and Mary Hamer were in effect using this convention, as she was the longest serving member of the band, having played piano (and danced) professionally at the Grafton Rooms before her interlude having children. Furthermore, she had previously led both the Bootle Palais de Danse band and the Embassy Bohemians – in both of which house bands Wilf had clearly been subordinate to her – and played a major role in shaping the Grafton Rooms' success through the Old-Tyme Nights. Nonetheless, and as we have already seen, very few women were playing professionally in Liverpool during the 1930s, never mind leading a popular all-male band.

---

[158] Clive Garner to Mike Brocken (October 1997); undergraduate seminar, Institute of Popular Music (University of Liverpool).

[159] Mary Hamer's characterisation of herself as a 'lady', rather than a 'woman', also suggests an insistence on respectability, with 'lady' signifying genteel respectability in the 1930s. (She was, of course, referring back to an era that pre-dated the later feminist politicisation of the term.)

[160] Mary Hamer, cited from Jenkins, *'Let's Go Dancing'*, 42.

The reference to unsolicited external applications regarding the vacant bandleader's job at the Grafton offers further testimony to the fame of both Wilf Hamer's Band and the Grafton Rooms at the time. The chance to lead a popular band in one of the region's most celebrated dance halls must have been appealing to many leading (male) musicians and it would make interesting reading if any such applications became known. We must also remember, of course, that Munro was Mary Hamer's brother-in-law, and that other band members were also relatives. Although it is possible that Munro might have been at least partly motivated (at a time of high mass unemployment, when poverty was widespread) to help a newly widowed member of his family, as a professional entertainments businessperson, he must also have recognised that there was nobody better qualified than she to take over her husband's former position. Mary Hamer already held nearly two decades of professional experience. Furthermore, there was now a 'novelty' value to the band – which, given Mary Hamer's abilities, would most certainly be good for business.

Both Mary Hamer's own initial nervousness about taking over the band and the pockets of internal male resistance might have been prompted by more than entitlement, misogyny, and musical considerations. Her position as woman leading an otherwise all-male band was extremely rare; her position as a woman leading an otherwise all-male band who also happened to be a single mother was even more so. In October 1936, when Mary Hamer officially took up her new position as leader on the Grafton Rooms' bandstand, she was also a widow and mother to a four-year-old, two-year-old, and three-month-old. Thus, she faced considerable practical barriers to pursuing a career that largely took place during unsocial and distinctly not family-friendly hours. In the 1980s she recollected how very challenging her situation was:

> All three boys were under four. The baby was only two weeks old when they took his dad away. I must admit I enjoyed the job. It was hard, it was very hard – late nights. The domestic side of my life was very difficult. It was very awkward having three children under five.[161]

She solved this domestic problem by employing a nanny.

Despite any initial reservations, Mary Hamer led the band very successfully throughout the remainder of the 1930s. For example, by May 1937 she was already confident enough with her position as bandleader to accept the band's now well-established summer season at the Queen's Dance Hall in Rhyl. She might have been a little relieved to note that renowned Liverpool dancer, competitor, and teacher Billy Martin, who had joined the Grafton staff back in

---

[161] Mary Hamer, cited from Jenkins, *'Let's Go Dancing'*, 41.

September 1935, had agreed to take over the management of the Queen's Dance Hall for that summer season; perhaps to support (and to dance with) Mary. While Mary Hamer was leading her band in Rhyl, back at the Grafton Rooms Munro replaced Mrs Hamer and her Boys with Bob Pendleton's band from the Ashton-under-Lyne Palais. It was only a summer season booking and when Mary Hamer and her Boys returned to the Grafton Rooms in the autumn, they continued to present high quality varied performances throughout the winter months.

During Mrs Wilf Hamer and her Band's summer residency in Rhyl and occasionally through the winter season as well, a variety of guest bands also appeared at the Grafton, which in fact aided Mary Hamer as a working mother. Clive Garner informed Mike Brocken that (to paraphrase) even though Mary loved her work, she was usually glad of the break and the opportunity to spend time with her sons.[162] However, so versatile were Mrs Hamer's Boys that they were usually on hand for the many dancing competitions and the programme of special events at the venue. For example, in the autumn/winter season of 1937 alone, she led the band at the Lancashire and Cheshire dance competition in October, at the 100 guineas Mecca Gold Cup event in December, and at the Christmas Galas. These latter two events were advertised in the local press as 'going with a swing' and Grafton manager Munro detected that 'swing music was once again to come in vogue [reaching] its zenith during the second great war years'.[163] Such comments concerning changing and developing genres inform us of Mary Hamer's versatility as a bandleader, pianist, and dancer, as she and her band certainly kept up with the changing musical times.

Mary Hamer's success leading the Grafton Rooms house band is also reflected in the number of BBC broadcasts they made. This is significant as the BBC was very particular about the quality and styles of dance bands which were broadcast over the radio and the venues from which they transmitted, as discussed in Section 2. The quality of both Mrs Wilf Hamer and Her Band and the Grafton Rooms as a venue is indicated by the frequency with which they were invited to make BBC broadcasts throughout the later 1930s. Mary Hamer was well known enough in London for her to become one of the first dance bands musicians from the English provinces to make an early television broadcast for the BBC from Alexandra Palace in 1937.[164] The BBC had commenced television broadcasts on 2 November 1936 and wanted to connect with artists representing the regions; in many ways Mary Hamer was an obvious choice. She recalled in later years: 'At that time, I did a television

---

[162] Garner to Brocken (October 1997).   [163] Munro, *Dancing Mad*, 156.
[164] Jenkins, *'Let's Go Dancing'*, 53–54.

broadcast. I thought the man had gone mad. I said, "I've done my face", he said, "We'll fix your face". I did it from Alexandra Palace in 1937, covered in [what was most likely a green coloured] make up.[165] I was the first one, he told me, from the provinces.'[166]

Although the majority of Mrs Wilf Hamer and her Band's BBC radio broadcasts were made from the Grafton Rooms, they also broadcast from a number of other dance halls when they appeared as a guest band. On 14 June 1938, for example, *The Radio Times* alerted radio listeners that Mrs Wilf Hamer and her Band 'will play to you from the Queen's Dance Hall at Rhyl this evening at 6.30 [pm]'. *The Radio Times* also featured a photograph of Mrs Wilf Hamer seated at a grand piano surrounded by her nine bandsmen and enthused that: 'This band has broadcast on several occasions under its present conductor, Mrs. Wilf Hamer, who took it over after the tragic death of her husband. She is a talented pianist and singer, and has several times broadcast under her own name, Marie Daly.'[167]

This live broadcast was made when Mary Hamer and her Boys returned to the North Wales resort of Rhyl for an incredibly successful summer season during 1938. Finding time to visit North Wales to watch his favourite bandleader in action; Munro later declared:

> During this busy summer season, I occasionally visited Rhyl, where our resident band with Mrs Wilf Hamer and Billy Martin were carrying on the Grafton dancing tradition at the Queen's Dance Hall. [by now] The band had many broadcasts to its credit, and were succeeding in making the North Wales Coast almost as dance conscious as Merseyside. There were competitions and demonstrations [there] by the same celebrities who had appeared at the Grafton.[168]

While Mrs Hamer and her Boys were away, back in Liverpool Bob Pendleton's band once more deputised and the Grafton Rooms also welcomed visiting guest bands such as those led by Ray Noble, Roy Fox, Ambrose, Joe Loss, and Jack Hylton.[169] All the guest bands were great attractions at the Grafton that summer. In fact, so well-liked were these popular music bandleaders of the late 1930s that keen dancer Audrey McKinnell informed us that as a young woman she recalled people going to the Grafton at this time 'as much to listen to these famous dance bands, as they did to dance to them'.[170]

---

[165] At this time heavy green make up was used to get the correct shading balance for TV.
[166] Mary Hamer, cited from Jenkins, *'Let's Go Dancing'*, 53–54.
[167] Anonymous, *The Radio Times*, Issue 767 (10 June 1938), 39, http://genome.ch.bbc.co.uk/page/662e2601b66744699d4579331fca5411 (last accessed 14 June 2023).
[168] Munro, *Dancing Mad*, 158–159.   [169] *Ibid.*, 156.   [170] Source: Audrey McKinnell.

Leadership Style and Strategies

Mary Hamer's success as bandleader is accountable to her skills as both a musician and a dancer, as well as her common sense and good professional judgement in gauging what genres and subgenres of popular music were best to perform. As she explained in later life in relation to her approach to leading the band:

> Sometimes I think there was no-one better qualified […] because when at times when I wasn't there, something would go wrong […] because the men in the band hadn't the same interest. […] I would try and give the people a good time and play the dances they wanted, like plenty of Paul Jones and the party dances […] the band were never keen on playing those things. They wanted to play all the hot stuff and jives and what have you, and I used to say this is what they want. They only come out perhaps once every six months to dance and they were always very pleased, and they always had repeat dances which made the box office go up and that's really what I was concerned about, that it should be a success.[171]

Mary Hamer's comments here highlight contemporary tensions between the musical needs and expectations of dancers and those of dance band musicians. As already noted, musicians (influenced by jazz) often wanted to play around with the dances, particularly through experimenting with different tempos and through improvisation. Dancers, on the other hand, wanted the music played straight at steady tempos, as discussed in Section 2 and which Victor Silvester famously exploited through his 'strict tempo' recordings. Mary Hamer appears to have drawn on her own embodied experience as a highly accomplished dancer when conducting. It is highly likely that she and Wilf Hamer shared the same concerns about putting the physical needs of the dancers first and curbing any enthusiasm towards improvisation or playing with the tempo, which he had expanded upon in his (cited earlier) article for the *Liverpool Echo* discussed in Section 4; they no doubt cross-influenced each other's band leadership approaches.

All-Girl Bands

Mary Hamer's initial concerns that a woman leading an otherwise all-male band would be seen as unusual are understandable, as this was an uncommon situation during the 1930s. It was not true, however, that women bandleaders were a rarity during this period, as the interwar years and into the Second World War were truly a golden age of all-'girl' bands, as they were known at the time.[172] It was the highly

---

[171] Mary Hamer, cited from Jenkins, *'Let's Go Dancing'*, 42.
[172] For a seminal study of all-girl bands in the United States, see Sherrie Tucker, *Swing Shift: 'All-Girl' Bands of the 1940s* (Durham: Duke University Press, 2000).

masculine – often macho – environment of much popular music performance, and the venues in which popular music was performed, that often made it difficult from women to integrate into mixed bands.[173] With the notable exception of singers, women faced nearly impenetrable gender barriers when trying to join male-dominated bands. Those that did often found their reputations irrevocably damaged; hence the probable motivation to emphasis Mary Hamer's respectability through the adoption of 'Mrs Wilf Hamer' as her professional name following her husband's death. In opposition to the difficulties routinely encountered when trying to join mixed bands, women began to form their own bands. This trend of all-girl bands – immortalised by Sweet Sue and her Society Syncopators in Billy Wilder's 1959 hit movie *Some Like It Hot* – was a particularly marked feature of interwar popular music in North America and throughout Europe. In the UK, Ivy Benson (1913–1993) – who managed to maintain an all-woman swing band for over 35 years – is probably the most famous example of a British woman bandleader.

The vast majority of women bandleaders (both in the UK and internationally) during the first half of the twentieth century worked with all-women bands. Therefore, what also marks out Mary Hamer as different was that she worked with an all-male band. Two other (more well-known) examples of women leading all-male bands in the UK during the interwar period are the famous ballroom dancer, Josephine Bradley, who led an all-male ensemble known as Josephine Bradley and her Ballroom Orchestra,[174] and the aforementioned Ennis Parkes, the former wife of famous bandleader, Jack Hylton, who, as discussed earlier, led the relatively short-lived Mrs Jack Hylton's Band during the mid-1930s. We are not currently aware of any other examples of women leading professional all-male bands during this period.[175]

Image

Her difference to the majority of other women bandleaders was emphasised by Mary Hamer's clothes and image. Most women bandleaders, such as Josephine Bradley, for example, generally cultivated an ultra-glamorous public image –

---

[173] See Linda Dahl, *Stormy Weather: The Music and Lives of a Century of Jazzwomen* (New York: Pantheon Books, 1984) and Nichole T. Rustin and Sherrie Tucker (eds.), *Big Ears: Listening for Gender in Jazz Studies* (Durham and London: Duke University Press, 2008).

[174] On Josephine Bradley, who was primarily a ballroom dancer rather than a musician, see her auto-biography, *Dancing through Life*.

[175] There may, of course, be other examples of hidden histories of women (such as Romana and her Men of Music in the United States) leading otherwise all-male dance bands in the UK during this period, which future research will reveal.

Figure 4 Josephine Bradley and Wellesley Smith appearing at the Grafton Rooms in 1931. Courtesy of Liverpool Central Library and Archives.

obviously influenced by the movie-stars of the age – appearing on the bandstand in a series of glamorous evening gowns, with elaborate hair and make-up (see Figure 4).

In the United States, Ina Ray Hutton (1916–1984, bandleader of the famous all-girl band The Melodears) was an important trend setter in this field, and many women bandleaders emulated her glamorous image. Mary Hamer, in contrast, often dressed in the same clothes as her bandsmen and usually wore a dickey-bow (see Figure 5).

Figure 5 Mary Hamer and her boys in their summer attire (1937). Courtesy of Liverpool Central Library and Archives.

Audrey McKinnell has recollected that:

> Mary Hamer would dress very smartly, often wore a 'dickie bow' and at times a kind of trouser suit – almost a bit military, really. It gave her a particular 'look' and I've wondered since whether she did it deliberately to make her look a bit masculine, leading an all-male band and all that.[176]

---
[176] Interview with Audrey McKinnell (5 March 2015).

It is highly likely that Audrey is on to something here. It is apparent from extant photographs of Mary Hamer and Her Band that she styled herself to fit in with the other members. Dressing the same as the men allowed her to minimise her feminine sexuality, and also allowed her visually to fit in with them much more than had she appeared in a slinky evening dress. As Mary Hamer had to negotiate the very real complication of taking on a traditionally male leadership role – quite literally leading an all-male group, at a time when men were used to leading in both public and private life – and perhaps especially given the pockets of initial internal male resistance from within the band itself – it may well be that minimising her sexuality via dress also helped her to reduce any perceived threat that a woman leading an all-male band might have posed.

The Second World War and Beyond: Dancing through the Blitz and Blackout

When the Second World War broke out in 1939, Mary Hamer sent her three sons out of Liverpool to a boarding school in the country for safety. Liverpool was heavily blitzed, and, as she later recalled, she felt 'so frightened for them'.[177] She remained in Liverpool to lead the band, however, travelling back and forth to the Grafton Rooms from the Wirral peninsular.[178] During the summer of 1939 the Grafton Rooms closed for redecoration and the laying of a brand-new dance floor. The venue re-opened on August Bank Holiday with a new Canadian maple floor laid on top of the existing oak sprung floor and preparations for the new autumn and winter dancing season were already well under way. However, by September 1939 war had been declared and all places of entertainment closed; this unpopular declaration from the government remained in place for only two weeks. When the order was given across Merseyside to re-open dance halls, they were packed with young people dancing the night away. Malcolm Munro later confirmed that 'house full' notices became the order of the day, as all the ballrooms were packed nightly; 'we [at the Grafton] just opened the doors at 7pm, later at 6.30pm and closed the evening at 10pm, a little later at 11pm and that is how we went on for about five years.'[179] Mary Hamer, with Munro's backing, was intent on leading her 'Boys' no matter what. As Nott has commented, 'At the Grafton Rooms [...] the management advertised itself as "Liverpool's Bombproof Ballroom" and it had a policy of carrying on dancing during alerts and barrages, with Mrs Wilf Hamer conducting the orchestra wearing her tin hat during air raids'.[180] When she had initially returned to Liverpool from North Wales, she experienced a personnel problem: the

---

[177] Mary Hamer, cited from Jenkins, *'Let's Go Dancing'*, 42.   [178] Source: George Hamer.
[179] Munro, *Dancing Mad*, 162.   [180] Nott, *Going to the Palais*, 70.

band's ranks were being depleted by conscription. Most of her band were of military age with others required for work of national importance.

In fact, Mary Hamer's band contained only one member over the conscription age: the trombone player and percussionist Harry Fisher, who had been a member of every Grafton house band since the venue had opened in 1924. The Grafton management held discussions, and it was agreed by the Board that, should it become impossible to recruit new band members of the required standard, Mary Hamer and Harry Fisher were to continue as a duo to provide dancers with entertainment and recreation. Whether this decision was made via expediency or convenience will never truly be known, yet perhaps the Grafton management might have thought that during wartime restrictions and with declining audiences a female pianist and an ageing drummer would be a far cheaper prospect than a full dance band; the idea appears to have stemmed from Fred Weisker. Munro later wrote:

> Evidently he could foresee what great profits would accrue if we had to pay for only two musicians instead of a band of ten [. . .] Subsequently I secured a nominal wage rate of £30 per week for the 'orchestra of eight pieces' with the addition of 50% of the monthly profits. Profit sharing in show business was generally accepted in World War One.[181]

Naturally, the profit-sharing concept was soon anathema to the Board of Directors when attendances at the Grafton surprisingly grew rather than diminished. According to Munro the Grafton accounts were then rigged so that the musicians were receiving a share of very little and 'when the profits did begin to soar about the middle of 1940 with the enormously increased business, he [Weisker] then scrapped the scheme and went back to the plan of paying the orchestra on a weekly rate, at that time £65 per week [Munro means per band, not per head!]'.[182] One cannot help but think that having a female bandleader played into the hands of the greedy Grafton management – despite there being a woman on the Board of Directors. The treatment of these professional musicians was indeed shameful. During the summer of 1940 Mary Hamer's Band were in fact playing to record breaking crowds with men of all nationalities being barracked in and around Merseyside. Guest appearances were also taking place with bandleaders such as Ken (Snakehips) Johnson, Joe Loss, Oscar Rabin, Harry Parry, Jack Jackson, and Ambrose amongst others, all bringing bands to play. Oscar Rabin's Band proved to be a great success and he returned as guest bandleader several times during the course of the war.

The nights of Friday 20th and Saturday 21st December 1940 were memorable in entirely other ways, however. Soon after 6pm the air raid sirens in Liverpool

---

[181] Munro, *Dancing Mad*, 164.　[182] *Ibid.*

began. The raids continued until 5am each of the following mornings. On each of these two evenings only a few dancers had paid to get into the Grafton – scarcely 100 on each night – and on Saturday 21st at about 6.30pm – just as the orchestra had started to play a bomb fell on the Olympia Theatre, which adjoined the Grafton Rooms. Malcolm Munro recalled:

> The blast took half the asbestos sheets from the Grafton roof and the flying pieces of shrapnel went through the plaster ceiling and marked the ballroom floor right across in a straight line just in front of the bandstand. Mrs Wilf Hamer, who was conducting the orchestra, and the boys dived headfirst under the grand piano and thus escaped serious injury. The Grafton roof had to be covered the next day with tarpaulin sheets until it was repaired with a new roof.[183]

Although on this occasion the show did not effectively 'go on', at least Mary Hamer and her Boys were able to escape serious injury. Popular entertainment continued to flourish in Liverpool throughout the Second World War, when the Grafton Rooms (who would accept any currency during that time) became a particularly favourite haunt with visiting American GIs and Australian soldiers based in Liverpool.

Ballroom in the Era of Rock 'n' Roll: Leading the Band into the 1950s

Mary Hamer's prestigious association with the BBC continued after the Second World War. For instance, *Melody Maker* proclaimed in May 1947 that the 'BBC introduces Northern Palais radio series starting with Mrs. Wilf Hamer and her Band from Liverpool's Grafton Rooms'.[184] The Grafton Rooms also continued to flourish as Liverpool's premier venue for ballroom dancing in the period directly following the Second World War, as exemplified through their luxurious 1949 souvenir programme (see Figure 6).

Mary Hamer left the Grafton Rooms for around two years in 1948/49.[185] During this time she briefly ran her own Star Ballroom in Wallasey.[186] Whilst she was away from the Grafton Rooms, the house band was led by Norman Rouse, who had been an original band member and arranger.[187] According to George Hamer, Munro persuaded Mary Hamer to return to the Grafton Rooms. Following her return, she continued to lead the band well into the 1950s, when the ballroom era eventually started to give way to Rock 'n' Roll. In later times, all three of her sons played in the band, as and when their National Service

---

[183] *Ibid.*, 168.   [184] Anonymous, *Melody Maker*, Vol. 14. No. 3 (May 1947), n.p.
[185] Munro, *Dancing Mad*, 128.   [186] Source: George Hamer.
[187] 'Famous the World Over', Grafton Rooms Souvenir Programme (1949); Liverpool Central Library and Archives, Shelf Mark: H793.33 GRA.

Figure 6 'Famous the World Over', The Grafton Rooms Souvenir Programme (1949). Courtesy of Liverpool Central Library and Archives.

commitments permitted. According to Munro and other family members, Mrs Wilf Hamer's Band disbanded in January 1956 or 1957. However, according to local journalist Stan Woolley in interview with Mary Hamer's eldest son, Ian, 'Mrs Wilf Hamer [. . .] continued to front the band at the Grafton until 1958'.[188] After Mary Hamer's band stopped playing at the Grafton Rooms, she, as George Hamer has shared with us, did not continue working, or even (beyond the

---

[188] Stan Woolley, 'The Hamers – and all that jazz at the Grafton'; unmarked and undated local Liverpool newspaper clipping, Hamer-Munro family archives (probably late 1980s or early 1990s).

occasional family party) playing the piano. George believes that this was largely due to the profound effect which the death of her second husband – John Howard, a local businessman, whom she had married in 1948 – had on her. He died in 1959, at the age of only forty-nine; shortly after her band finally folded. Thus, she suffered a double loss.

The Grafton Rooms continued to play an intrinsic part in Liverpool's subsequent popular music scenes, notably including both Merseybeat and country music in the 1960s. Whilst dance halls were closing down in droves all over the UK, the Grafton Rooms, as Nott has observed, was 'one of the most resilient'.[189] In the 1970s, the venue became an important disco. It also played a significant part in the 1980s post-punk indie scene, where local bands would play to large audiences. In 1999 a TV 'fly-on-the-wall' documentary was made there. The Grafton Rooms stumbled on into the twenty-first century, with a comedy club mooted in 2008.[190] The building is still standing though not currently in use.

6 Conclusion: Gender, Genre, and Looking beyond the Beatles

All three of Mary Hamer's sons went on to become professional jazz musicians in their own right: her middle son, Stewart, played drums and trumpet, and her youngest son, George, played the clarinet. Her eldest son, Ian Hamer (1932–2006), is probably the most famous today, as he became a renowned jazz trumpeter and session artist, even providing the well-known trumpet solos on the Beatles' 1966 album, *Revolver*. The Beatles reference, however, sadly also reminds us of the prevalence for popular music histories of Liverpool to focus on them to the virtual exclusion of all the other varied forms of popular music which have also flourished in the city, particularly when they involve women as active, rather than passive, agents. As and when Mary Hamer is currently remembered in wider popular music history, it is generally in relation to her more well-known eldest son. In the online biographical entry for Ian Hamer in the National Jazz Archive's website, for instance, John Rosie notes that 'Hamer was part of a musical family and played in his mother Mary Daly Hamer's big band with his brothers Stuart and George, while his father, Wilf Hamer, was a successful bandleader'.[191]

Beyond the deep-seated trend for popular music histories of Liverpool to focus upon the Beatles to the virtual exclusion of all the other varied forms of popular

---

[189] Nott, *Going to the Palais*, 93.

[190] Anonymous, 'End of an Era as Legendary Liverpool Club the Grafton Closes', Liverpool Echo (18 October 2008), available at: End of an era as legendary Liverpool club The Grafton closes–Liverpool Echo (last accessed 20 June 2023).

[191] John Rosie, 'Ian Hamer (1932–2006)', The National Jazz Archive Online; available at: Ian Hamer (nationaljazzarchive.org.uk) (last accessed 14 June 2023).

music which have flourished in the city before, after, and convergent with them, the reasons for Mary Hamer's almost total erasure are complex but central amongst them are gender and genre. As has been discussed, the participation of women, with the exception of singers, within jazz and dance band music has itself been marginalised, whilst academic studies of these genres have tended to privilege hot American jazz and denigrate sweet British dance band music. As Tackley has astutely observed, British dance music and 'symphonic syncopation' have been 'frequently written off as inauthentic white imitations'.[192] Although undoubtedly working within the 'sweet' British dance band music tradition, it was Mary Hamer's own embodied experience as a dancer, as we have seen, which guided her approach to dance band leadership – ensuring that the dances were played in a style most appropriate to dancing – rather than any musical deficiencies or lack of interest. Mary Hamer's activities are even further hidden from view by the tendency of those studies of British dance band music which do exist to focus upon London.

The extraordinary career of Mary Hamer deserves closer examination than that which we have been able to offer here. From her time directing the Bootle Palais de Danse band and the Embassy Bohemians and through the twenty years that she led Mrs Wilf Hamer's Band at the Grafton Rooms, she was acknowledged as one of the most talented, important, and influential bandleaders active in Liverpool and Merseyside, and was also, as we have seen, well known more widely, definitely including in London. Also respected as a highly accomplished dancer and pianist, with Malcolm Munro and Wilf Hamer she co-led the Old-Tyme dancing revival at the Grafton Rooms. By taking the first steps to uncover her hidden popular music history, we have sought to offer a revisionist counter-narrative which challenges the view that sweet British dance music is of little worth, points to the rich dance band music cultures which flourished throughout the UK beyond London, and, in centring Liverpool, shine a light upon one of the city's vibrant popular music scenes before the Beatles. We also offer an account which places a woman – and one who was equally musician *and* dancer – at the heart.

---

[192] Parsonage, *The Evolution of Jazz in Britain*, xi.

Bibliography

Unpublished, Archival, and Ethnographic Sources

The Hamer-Munro Family Archives (collection of original photographs, newspaper clippings, and assorted memorabilia from the Grafton Rooms, including programmes, dance cards, brochures, and publicity materials).

Liverpool Central Library and Archives (original photographs and souvenir programmes).

Malcolm Munro, *Dancing Mad: An Autobiographical Dancing Diary* (unpublished, c1968).

Original interviews with Clive Garner, Audrey McKinnell, George Hamer, Henry Mooney, and Margaret MacKennon.

Published Sources

Abra, Allison, *Dancing in the English Style: Consumption, Americanisation and National Identity in Britain, 1918–50* (Manchester: Manchester University Press, 2017).

Anonymous, 'Liverpool's Biggest Dance Hall Opens: A Real Palais de Danse for Merseyside', *Liverpool Echo* (9 February 1924), n.p.

Anonymous, 'Pas de Trios', *Liverpool Echo* (12 February 1924), n.p.

Anonymous, 'Old-Time Enthusiasm', *Liverpool Echo* (1932), n.p.

Anonymous, 'Day to Day', *Birmingham Daily Post* (November 1933), n.p.

Anonymous, 'Liverpool', *Tune Times* (October 1934), 66.

Anonymous, Untitled, *Dance Band Diaries* (14 December 1935), 3.

Anonymous, Untitled, *Dance Band Diaries* (21 December 1935), 5.

Anonymous, *Radio Pictorial* (week of 7th February 1936), n.p.

Anonymous, 'Stop Press', *Melody Maker*, Vol. 7, No. 9 (18 July 1936), 2.

Anonymous, *The Radio Times*, Issue 767 (10 June 1938), 39.

Anonymous, *Melody Maker*, Vol. 14, No. 3 (May 1947).

Anonymous, 'End of an Era as Legendary Liverpool Club the Grafton Closes', *Liverpool Echo* (18 October 2008); available online at End of an era as legendary Liverpool club The Grafton closes – Liverpool Echo.

Bradley, Josephine, *Dancing through Life* (London: Hollis & Carter, 1947).

Brocken, Michael, *Other Voices: Hidden Histories of Liverpool's Popular Music Scenes, 1930s–1970s* (Farnham: Ashgate, 2010).

Brocken, Michael, *The 21st Century Legacy of the Beatles: Liverpool and Popular Music Heritage Tourism* (Farnham: Ashgate, 2015).

Brocken, Michael, and Jeff Daniels, *Gordon Stretton, Black British Transoceanic Jazz Pioneer – A New Jazz Chronicle* (London: Lexington, 2018).

Buckland, Theresa, *Society Dancing: Fashionable Bodies in England, 1870–1920* (Basingstoke: Palgrave Macmillan, 2011).

Buckland, Theresa, 'How the Waltz Was Won', *Dance Research: The Journal of the Society for Dance Research*, Vol. 36, No. 1 (Summer 2018), 1–32 and Vol. 36, No. 2 (Winter 2018), 138–172.

Cohen, Sara, *Decline, Renewal and the City in Popular Music Culture: Beyond the Beatles* (Farnham: Ashgate, 2007).

Cottrell, Stephen, *The Saxophone* (New Haven: Yale University Press, 2013).

Cresswell, Tim, '"You Cannot Shake that Shimmie Here": Producing Mobility on the Dance Floor', *Cultural Geographies*, Vol. 13 (2006), 55–77.

Dahl, Linda, *Stormy Weather: The Music and Lives of a Century of Jazzwomen* (New York: Pantheon Books, 1984).

Godbolt, Jim, *A History of Jazz in Britain, 1919–1950*, Revised Edition (London: Northway Books, 2005).

Grossberg, Lawrence, 'Is There a Fan in the House? The Affective Sensibility of Fandom', in Lisa A. Lewis (ed.), *The Adoring Audience: Fan Culture and Popular Media* (London: Routledge, 1992), 50–65.

Hamer, Wilf, 'Dancing on Merseyside: The Band's Point of View; Getting the Atmosphere; The Ideal Combination', *Liverpool Echo* (mid-1930s; Hamer-Munro Archives), n.p.

Jenkins, Henry, '"Strangers No More We Sing": Filking and the Social Construction of the Science Fiction Fan Community', in Lisa A. Lewis (ed.), *The Adoring Audience: Fan Culture and Popular Media* (London: Routledge, 1992), 208–236.

Jenkins, Tricia, *'Let's Go Dancing': Dance Band Memories of 1930s Liverpool*, Liverpool Sound Series (Liverpool: University of Liverpool Press/Institute of Popular Music, 1994).

Leonard, Marion, and Robert Strachan, *The Beat Goes On: Liverpool, Popular Music and the Changing City* (Liverpool: Liverpool University Press, 2010).

Nott, James J., *Music for the People: Popular Music and Dance in Interwar Britain* (Oxford: Oxford University Press, 2002).

Nott, James J., 'Contesting Popular Dancing and Dance Music in Britain during the 1920s', *Cultural and Social History*, Vol. 10, No. 3 (2013), 439–456.

Nott, James J., *Going to the Palais: A Social and Cultural Study of Dancing and Dance Halls in Britain, 1918–1960* (Oxford: Oxford University Press, 2015).

Parsonage, Catherine [Tackley], *The Evolution of Jazz in Britain, 1880–1935* (Aldershot: Ashgate, 2005).

Parsonage, Catherine [Tackley], and Kathy Dyson, 'The History of Women in Jazz in Britain', in Patricia Adkins Chiti (ed.), *Women in Jazz/Donne in Jazz* (Rome: Editore Columbo, 2007), 129–140.

Priestley, J. B., *English Journey* (London: Heinemann, 1934).

Pugh, Martin, *'We Danced All Night': A Social History of Britain between the Wars* (London: Bodley Head, 2008).

Rosie, John, 'Ian Hamer (1932–2006)', The National Jazz Archive Online; available at: Ian Hamer (nationaljazzarchive.org.uk) (last accessed 14 June 2023).

Rustin, Nicole T., and Sherrie Tucker (eds.), *Big Ears: Listening for Gender in Jazz Studies* (Durham: Duke University Press, 2008).

Silvester, Victor, *Dancing Is My Life: The Autobiography of Victor Silvester* (London: Heinemann, 1958).

Spencer, Frank and Peggy, *Come Dancing* (London: WH Allen, 1968).

Tucker, Sherrie, *Swing Shift: 'All-Girl' Bands of the 1940s* (Durham: Duke University Press, 2000).

Wilson, Jen, *Freedom Music: Wales, Emancipation and Jazz, 1850–1950* (Cardiff: University of Wales Press, 2019).

Zimring, Rishona, *Social Dance and the Modernist Imagination in Interwar Britain* (Farnham: Ashgate, 2013).

Acknowledgements

We wish to thank the many people who have supported us whilst we worked upon this project. Our heartfelt thanks go to the late Audrey McKinnell, who first sparked our joint interest in Mary Hamer and the Grafton Rooms. Tremendous thanks are also due to the members of Mary Hamer and Malcolm Munro's family who met with us, shared their memories of her, and granted us generous access to the Hamer-Munro private family archives, especially her son the late George Hamer, great niece Margaret MacKennon, and grandson Henry Mooney. We are grateful to Lauren Lavery, Research Officer at Liverpool Central Library and Archives, who kindly helped us with sourcing original photographs and programmes. Our thanks also go to Rhiannon Mathias, series editor of CUP's Women in Music Elements, and to Kate Brett at Cambridge University Press for her encouragement. We also thank our own families for all their loving support during the long gestation period of this project. As far as we know, Mary Hamer is not a relative of Laura's. All images are reproduced courtesy of Liverpool Central Library and Archives.

In memory of Robert Douglas Hamer

Cambridge Elements

Women in Music

Rhiannon Mathias
Bangor University

Dr. Rhiannon Mathias is Lecturer and Music Fellow in the School of Music and Media at Bangor University. She is the author of a number of women in music publications, including *Lutyens, Maconchy, Williams and Twentieth-Century British Music: A Blest Trio of Sirens* (2012), and gives frequent conference presentations, public lectures and radio broadcasts on the topic. She is also the editor of the Routledge Handbook on *Women's Work in Music*, a publication which arose from the First International Conference on Women's Work in Music (Bangor University, 2017), which she instigated and directed. The success of the first conference led to her directing a second conference in 2019.

About the Series

Elements in Women in Music provides an exciting and timely resource for an area of music scholarship which is undergoing rapid growth. The subject of music, women and culture is widely researched in the academy, and has also recently become the focus of much public debate in mainstream media.

This international series will bring together many different strands of research on women in classical and popular music. Envisaged as a multimedia digital 'stage' for showcasing new perspectives and writing of the highest quality, the series will make full use of online materials such as music sound links, audio and/or film materials (e.g. performances, interviews – with permission), podcasts and discussion forums relevant to chosen themes.

The series will appeal primarily to music students and scholars, but will also be of interest to music practitioners, industry professionals, educators and the general public.

Cambridge Elements⚌

Women in Music

Elements in the Series

Grażyna Bacewicz, The 'First Lady of Polish Music'
Diana Ambache

Leokadiya Kashperova
Graham Griffiths

Julie Reisserová (1888–1938)
Jean-Paul C. Montagnier

Bandleader Mrs Mary Hamer and Her Boys: Popular Music and Dance Cultures in Interwar Liverpool
Laura Hamer and Michael Brocken

A full series listing is available at: www.cambridge.org/ewim

For EU product safety concerns, contact us at Calle de José Abascal, 56–1°, 28003 Madrid, Spain or eugpsr@cambridge.org.

www.ingramcontent.com/pod-product-compliance
Lightning Source LLC
LaVergne TN
LVHW020351260326
834688LV00045B/1667